Dam Good Sweet

Desserts to Satisfy Your Sweet Tooth, NEW ORLEANS STYLE

David Guas & Raquel Pelzel

The Taunton Press

Text © 2009 by David Guas
Photographs © 2009 by Ellen Silverman,
except for the following: p. 3 © 2009 Carl Rulis; pp. 9, 36,
109, 163 © 2009 Eugenia Uhl; p. 12 Library of Congress,
Prints & Photographs Division, Arnold Genthe Collection:
Negatives and Transparencies, Reproduction
Number LC-G391-T-1423; p. 83 Covert, *Loading Stacks of
Coffee*, c. 1917, Courtesy of the Louisiana State Museum,
Gift of the Chamber of Commerce of the New Orleans
Area; p. 115 courtesy C. S. Steen Syrup Mill, Inc.; p. 123
courtesy Ponchatoula Strawberry Festival; p. 141 Covert,
Creole Praline Department, Fuerst and Kraemer, Ltd., 1917,
Courtesy of the Louisiana State Museum, Gift of the
Chamber of Commerce of the New Orleans Area

All rights reserved.

The Taunton Press
Inspiration for hands-on living®

The Taunton Press, Inc., 63 South Main Street,
PO Box 5506, Newtown, CT 06470-5506
e-mail: tp@taunton.com

Editor: Carolyn Mandarano
Copy Editor: Tammalene Mitman
Indexer: Heidi Blough
Jacket and Interior Design: Carol Singer
Layout: Kimberly Shake
Photographers: Ellen Silverman, except where noted above
Food Stylist: Heidi Johannsen Stewart
Prop Stylist: Heather Chontos

Library of Congress Cataloging-in-Publication Data

Guas, David.
  DamGoodSweet : desserts to satisfy your sweet tooth
New Orleans style / David Guas and Raquel Pelzel.
     p. cm.
  Includes index.
  ISBN 978-1-60085-118-6
  1. Desserts. 2. Desserts--Louisiana--New
Orleans. I. Pelzel, Raquel. II. Title.
  TX773.G825 2009
  641.8'6--dc22

                                   2009016363

Printed in China
10 9 8 7 6 5 4 3 2 1

*To my wife Simone, whose creative
energy is never turned off and whose
passion for good sweets is inspiring.*

The following manufacturers/names appearing
in *DamGoodSweet* are trademarks:

A&P[SM], A&W®, Abita®, Balducci's®, Barq's®, Bud®,
Café du Monde®, Ceresota®, Coca Cola®, Community®,
Cracker Jack®, Crystal®, Diamond Crystal®, Dr. Pepper®,
Dufour®, E. Guittard®, French Market®, Ghirardelli®, Good
Humor®, Harley®, Heckers®, Honda®, Hundred Grand®, King
Arthur®, M&Ms®, Mahatma®, Maker's Mark®, Maldon®,
Milky Way®, Morton's®, Nielsen Massey®, Plugra®, Pomona's®,
Popeye's[SM], Raisin Bran®, Safeway[SM], Santa Lucia®, Sazerac®,
Silpat®, Slow Food®, Sno-Bliz®, SnoWizard®, Steen's™,
Sugar in the Raw®, Tabasco®, Technicolor®, Triscuits®,
Valrhona®, White Lily®

Acknowledgments

DAVID GUAS

Special thanks to Raquel Pelzel, whose ability to transfer my words, memories, stories, and recipes to paper is topnotch. To my mother and father, Linda and Mariano Guas, who gave me so many opportunities growing up in New Orleans and whose guidance continues to shape my career. To my two boys, Kemp and Spencer, who have still to this day never turned down a dessert of mine. To my Nan, whose generous donation allowed me to pursue my culinary schooling. To Aunt Boo, for never holding back and always telling it like it is. To Jeff Tunks, for giving me my first professional opportunity and for giving me such creative freedom in his kitchens for over ten years.

To The Taunton Press, for everyone's patience in working with me on this book and for taking the risk on signing my first book (you guys [Carolyn Mandarano] rock!). Thanks to Suvir Saran, who pushed me in the direction of writing a book and introduced me to Raquel (coauthor) and Angela (my agent), you are a dear friend. Angela Miller, the world's greatest agent, thank you for meeting with me at the Peninsula NYC to discuss my ideas. To Ellen Silverman, whose photographs brought to life my desserts and made me want to bake everything all over again.

RAQUEL PELZEL

David, thank you for inviting me to travel through time with you as you revisited your memories of growing up in New Orleans; for introducing me to the amazing stories, people, and sweets of Louisiana (and those burgers at Port of Call); for being so patient; and for never making fun of my mispronunciation of just about everything. Thanks to Simone, Kemp, and Spencer for letting David venture off on this journey for the last few years. A big thank you to David's family for nurturing him with so many lovely traditions and sweet recollections—Aunt Boo, I hope I get to meet you some day.

To Carolyn Mandarano, you got it from day one. Thank you for your gentle words, encouragement, and steadfast support. Thanks to Don Linn, Allison Hollett, Laurie Buckle, Katy Binder, Alison Wilkes, Carol Singer, and the whole Taunton team for your vision and enthusiasm. Ellen Silverman, Heidi Johannsen Stewart, and Heather Chontos: thank you for representing these recipes so beautifully—I have never seen a sexier chocolate pudding. Suvir Saran, thanks for the introduction, you're pretty damnsweet yourself. To Angela Miller, Sharon Bowers, and Jennifer Griffin, without your guidance and commitment we'd never be here.

Finally, to Matt, Julian, my Chicago and New Hampshire families, and my extended family of friends and neighbors in Brooklyn, thanks for helping me eat every recipe in this book. I expect reciprocation in full—how about we start with a nice red velvet cake? I'll bring the milk.

CONTENTS

Introduction

was no angel growing up in New Orleans, a city that caters more to debauchery than to chastity. At the ripe old age of 14 I'd break out of my bedroom window and sneak into the garage to "borrow" my dad's car, coasting in neutral until I was midway down the block before daring to turn on the ignition. I had a fake ID and routinely snuck off my high school's campus. I'd lie to my parents, fight with my sister, and be an all-around punk of a kid—and when I pushed mom and dad too far, they'd send me to Aunt Boo's in Abbeville, three hours west of New Orleans, where I could, according to Aunt Boo, have some good, clean fun and gain back my righteousness by making roux.

At Aunt Boo's house, the kitchen was sacred. It wasn't fancy, dressed up with polished copper pots and the like; it was functional. She had a few time-honored and blackened cast iron pots and skillets that she used for her gumbos and étouffées, a few baking pans, and a hard-working oven. I'd enter the kitchen and find her at the stove, a wooden spoon in one hand, a cold beer in the other, stirring up a pot of something that smelled so amazing I thought I'd died and gone to heaven. I took comfort in her kitchen, a place of order and rules that were not broken under any circumstances. She was the master and I her apprentice. It was my first taste of kitchen hierarchy.

Together, Aunt Boo and I made classic Louisiana dishes like shrimp Creole and a spicy redfish and tomato stew called coubeyon (say it: coo-BE-yawn with a silent "n" at the end). She taught me how to blacken fish, whip up her Nana's old-school banana bread, and make my first roux. Heck, she even gave me

my first cast iron pan. The most important lesson that I learned from her was that there's a time for fun, and a time to be serious, and cooking good, honest food was a serious matter. It was in her kitchen that the seeds for my future as a chef were sown.

I got my first break as a pastry chef at the age of 11, when I was hired to make sno-balls (New Orleans–style shaved ice) at an old storage room that had been converted into a sno-ball stand on Chef Menteur Highway. It was the first time I ever made something that other people paid to eat. Little did I know this was the beginning of my career in desserts.

After high school, I went to college and was home within two years—the party-going New Orleanian in me came out, and my studies suffered. I got a job slinging steak in a cheesesteak shop and quickly climbed the ranks from grill cook to manager. Once again, I discovered how satisfying it was to make other people happy. Making cheesesteaks wasn't glamorous, but it pointed me in the right direction: culinary school.

I was looking through the paper one day and saw an ad for Sclafani Cooking School in Metairie. All of a sudden it clicked—I knew this was what I wanted to do with my life. I learned about mother sauces, stocks, consommés, and how to season food; the whole pastry session was—at most—three days long!

When I went looking for a job, I started with Gerard Crozier, one of the premiere French chefs in the city. He hired me to work at his restaurant, but a few days later unhired me because the person whose job I was taking changed her mind. It was a tough break but actually a lucky one, too, because a few days later I went for an interview in the best kitchen in all of New

Orleans, at the Windsor Court Hotel. I applied for a job in the savory kitchen, but the only department hiring was pastry, so I interviewed for a job there with the executive pastry chef, Kurt Ebert, a master pastry chef from Germany. He wasn't too impressed with me, but I convinced him to hire me. It changed my life.

On my first day I got a crash course in how to hold a pastry bag by piping meringue onto 400 lemon tartlets, and I learned how to use a dough sheeter by making a seemingly never-ending supply of spicy cheese straws. I didn't catch my breath for nearly two years. Jeff Tunks, the Windsor's executive chef, would come to the pastry department in the basement and we'd shoot it for hours, him perched on a few 50-pound bags of flour and me piping, whisking, kneading, and rolling. He spoke elusively about a project he was involved with in Washington, D.C. He had his goons (a term I use lovingly to describe his sous-chefs), Cliff and Linton, take me out for billiards and Buds® and ask me all kinds of hypothetical questions, like would I leave town if the right job came along? I guess I answered the questions right because in February of 1998, I packed up and left New Orleans for the nation's capital to open a restaurant that would be known as DC Coast and to serve as its executive pastry chef.

Within seven years I had helped to open three more restaurants: TenPenh, Ceiba, and Acadiana, with me being the head of pastry for the whole family. To get inspiration for TenPenh, I went to Indonesia to learn about Southeast Asian sweets for the dessert menu. For Ceiba, a Cuban-influenced restaurant, I tapped into my Cuban heritage (my dad was born in Havana, though his mother is a native Louisianan) and traveled to Miami to hang with my Cuban cousins. I revisited the desserts I loved best from my hometown when I compiled recipes for the Louisiana-influenced menu at Acadiana. It opened just twelve days after Hurricane Katrina hit the Gulf Coast.

The neighborhoods I grew up in, New Orleans East (a part of the Ninth Ward), and my parents' home in Lakeview were nearly erased by Hurricane Katrina. It hit me hard. After Katrina, I was inundated with memories of New Orleans. It was then I knew I had to record and preserve not only the dessert recipes of the region but my memories, too.

DamGoodSweet is the culmination of these efforts. About two years ago I left my DC Coast family to start my own consulting business. And soon I will be opening my own bakeshop, where I'll showcase the flavors of New Orleans and the surrounding region.

Whether due to Katrina or for other reasons, like new real estate developments or older proprietors who choose to retire, many of New Orleans's institutions, including Lawrence's Bakery (also called Mr. Wedding Cake) in Gentilly on Elysian Fields Avenue and McKenzie's next to the A&P℠ in New Orleans East, have faded away. But many are thriving, like Hansen's, Hubig's, and Clancy's.

Writing this cookbook is a way for me to celebrate the restaurants, bakeries, and sweet shops that remain and thrive in New Orleans as well as to keep alive the traditions of long-gone institutions. *DamGoodSweet* is for my family, friends, and anyone who holds dear the traditions and institutions of this unique city.

OLD SCHOOL
N'awlins

Classic New Orleans Desserts

The recipes in this chapter are New Orleans down to their sugary cores. They should be on every New Orleans visitor's list: beignets at Café du Monde or Morning Call, bananas Foster at Brennan's, bread pudding from Galatoire's, and king cake, which makes an appearance on every New Orleanian's kitchen table during the Carnival season. I also included a couple you might never have heard of, like Calas Fried Rice Fritters, a fritter just about as popular as beignets during the 19th century. These are the iconic recipes of my New Orleans and the Deep South. They deserve to be remembered, celebrated, and most of all, enjoyed.

Buttermilk Beignets

(Say it: BEN-yayz)

⊰❦⊱ ⊰❦⊱ ⊰❦⊱ ⊰❦⊱ ⊰❦⊱ ⊰❦⊱ ⊰❦⊱ ⊰❦⊱ ⊰❦⊱ ⊰❦⊱ ⊰❦⊱ ⊰❦⊱

Up until I was about 12 years old, my parents took my sister, Tracy, and me to Easter service at the St. Louis Cathedral in Jackson Square. The only way they could keep us in check during mass was by bribing us to be good and quiet with promises of post-church beignets at Café du Monde across the street. We'd get so excited about the prospect of massive quantities of sugar that we probably would have done pretty much anything to ensure we got beignets before going home. Mom was a bit of a stickler when it came to sweets; I mean, at our house, Raisin Bran® was considered toeing the line of junk food! So you can only imagine how amped up we were at the mere prospect of real, honest-to-goodness fried dough piled sky-high with a mountain of powdered sugar.

Like good southern kids we were dressed to the nines—me in my blue blazer, khakis, and white oxfords, Tracy in her Easter dress—and Mom, like all the proper matriarchs, with an Easter hat perched on her head that had a wingspan of at least 18 inches. No sooner had the crispy-fried beignets arrived than our holiday best was coated in a dusting of white powder, as it was our tradition to see who could blow the snowy confectioners' sugar off of the mountain of beignets and onto the other the quickest. After we'd made a complete mess of ourselves, we'd get down to business and devour our crispy-fried beignets, still hot from the fryer and so amazingly tender.

⊰❦⊱ ⊰❦⊱ ⊰❦⊱ ⊰❦⊱ ⊰❦⊱ ⊰❦⊱ ⊰❦⊱ ⊰❦⊱ ⊰❦⊱ ⊰❦⊱ ⊰❦⊱ ⊰❦⊱

Buttermilk Beignets

¾ cup whole milk

1½ cups buttermilk

4 teaspoons active dry yeast

2½ tablespoons sugar

3½ cups bread flour plus extra for flouring work surface

½ teaspoon baking soda

¼ teaspoon salt

Peanut oil for frying

Confectioners' sugar for serving, as much as you think you'll need—then double that!

Heat the milk in a small saucepan over medium-high heat until small bubbles form at the surface. Remove from the heat, add the buttermilk, and then pour into a stand mixer bowl. Whisk in the yeast and the sugar and set aside for 5 minutes. Add the flour, baking soda, and salt, and mix on low speed, using a dough hook, until the dry ingredients are moistened, 3 to 4 minutes. Increase the mixer speed to medium and continue mixing until the dough forms a loose ball and is still quite wet and tacky, 1 to 2 minutes longer. Cover the bowl with plastic wrap and set the dough aside in a draft-free spot for 1 hour.

Pour enough peanut oil into a large pot to fill it to a depth of 3 inches and bring to a temperature of 375°F over medium heat (this will take about 20 minutes). Line a plate with paper towels and set aside.

Lightly flour your work surface and turn the dough out on it. Sprinkle the top of the dough with flour, gently press to flatten, fold it in half, and gently tuck the ends under to create a rough-shaped round. Dust again and roll the dough out into a ½-inch- to ⅓-inch-thick circle. Let the dough rest for 1 minute before using a chef's knife, a bench knife, or a pizza wheel to cut the dough into 1½-inch squares (you should get about 48).

Gently stretch a beignet lengthwise and carefully drop it into the oil. Add a few beignets (don't overcrowd them, otherwise the oil will cool down and the beignets will soak up oil and be greasy) and fry until puffed and golden brown, turning them often with a slotted spoon, for 2 to 3 minutes. Transfer to the prepared plate to drain while you cook the rest. Serve while still warm, buried under a mound of confectioners' sugar, with hot coffee on the side.

MAKES ABOUT 4 DOZEN BEIGNETS

→MAKE AHEAD The beignet dough can be made up to 8 hours in advance of frying. Line a baking sheet with parchment paper and spray it with nonstick cooking spray. After cutting the dough, place the beignets on the paper and place another greased sheet of parchment paper, sprayed-side down, on top. Wrap the entire baking sheet with plastic wrap and refrigerate. The beignets can be fried straight from the refrigerator.

Though nearly as many of the stalls at the French Market now sell T-shirts and curios as others do fresh fruit, vegetables, and seafood, at one time, the French Market was where all of New Orleans went for "making groceries." It's America's oldest public market and was built by the Spanish in 1791 (it was designed by a Frenchman) as an attempt to formalize shopping hours, control prices, and make the city a cleaner place. Long before the site was developed, the land that runs parallel to the Mississippi River was a trading spot for native Choctaw Indians as well as European settlers.

In 1812, the building was destroyed by a hurricane and was rebuilt one year later and called the Halles des Boucheries because it was the only place pre-Civil War where folks could legally purchase meat. It wasn't until the 1850s that the market acquired the name "French Market," perhaps because it was in the French part of town or because most of the butchers were French. In any case, the name stuck, and the French Market is now one of the most visited spots in all of New Orleans.

Café du Monde opened in the French Market in the early 1860s and is still open 24/7, 364 days a year, closing only for Christmas. It is certainly the most popular place to indulge in beignets (though I like the ones at Morning Call in Metairie, too).

The origin of the New Orleans–style beignet is somewhat unclear, with some insisting it was French Acadians who brought the tradition from Nova Scotia, while others insist it was Ursuline nuns who introduced the yeast-raised fritter to the city. No matter who commenced the tradition, beignets became a common companion to coffee (New Orleans was and still is a big coffee importer—see p. 83 for more about coffee), and by the mid-1700s they were prevalent in many New Orleans coffee houses. As a means to stretch out the coffee supply (first utilized by the Acadians on their trek from Nova Scotia to Louisiana and then during the Civil War when coffee was scarce), roasted endive root, aka chicory, was added to dark roasted beans. An appreciation for the slightly bitter-tinged brew stuck, and now there are few experiences that can trump the pairing of fresh-fried beignets with a chicory-spiked and steaming mug of café au lait.

Bananas Foster

People in New Orleans love to feel special. That's why they go to old-school restaurants where the same waiter who has served them for generations is on first-name terms with the family patriarch, children, and even grandchildren. The waiter knows how to make his diners happy, and when dining at Brennan's in the French Quarter, it's often with a grand finale of bananas Foster. Made tableside, by sautéing bananas in hot sugar, adding rum, and then lighting the whole deal on fire, it delivers big time on that "wow!" factor that comes with having something created right in front of your eyes. As a kid, I was completely mesmerized—you could have pushed a pin through me and I wouldn't have moved.

½ cup pecan pieces

½ cup packed dark brown sugar

¼ teaspoon ground cinnamon

2 tablespoons dark rum

1 tablespoon banana liqueur (or
½ teaspoon banana flavoring)

4 ripe bananas

3 tablespoons unsalted butter
Straight Up Vanilla Bean Ice
Cream (p. 110) for serving

Heat the oven to 325°F. Place the pecan pieces on a baking sheet and toast until fragrant, 7 to 8 minutes. Set aside to cool. Place the brown sugar and cinnamon in a small bowl and set next to your stovetop. Pour the rum and banana liqueur into a small cup.

Peel the bananas and slice them in half crosswise and then slice in half lengthwise so you end up with 16 segments. Melt the butter in a large skillet over medium-high heat. Once melted, add the sugar and cinnamon to the pan, stirring constantly until the sugar starts to bubble and melt, 30 seconds to 1 minute.

Place the bananas in the skillet and then add the pecans. Gently stir with a wooden spoon to coat the bananas and pecans with the sugar mixture, being careful not to smash or break the bananas. Continue to cook until the sauce becomes syrupy, about 2 minutes, and then add the rum and banana liqueur. Using a utility lighter or a long wooden match, ignite the alcohol and allow the flames to die down (if you have a gas cooktop, after adding the alcohol you can tilt the pan away from you and toward the flame to encourage the alcohol to ignite). Divide the bananas Foster between four bowls, top with ice cream, and serve.

SERVES 4

VARIATION

DAD'S FAMOUS BAKED BANANAS

My dad was famous in our family for his take on bananas Foster: baked bananas. When I was a kid, I liked to think that because of his Cuban heritage Dad once ate a dish like this in Havana as a boy, perhaps made with ripe plantains in place of bananas. Without fail, once my sister and I got wind that Dad was making his bananas, we'd race into the kitchen and watch him throw together this simple yet completely awesome dish: Heat the oven to 375°F. Place 3 bananas, peeled and halved lengthwise, into a baking dish. Sprinkle the bananas with a generous handful of light brown sugar, sprinkle with cinnamon, and top with a few knobs of unsalted butter. Bake until the bananas are caramelized and coated with a golden brown layer of sugar syrup, 20 to 25 minutes, basting occasionally. Serve warm or at room temperature with ice cream or crêpes.

New Orleans has a history with bananas. From the mid-19th century, the city was a major port of entry for bananas and other tropical imports (like coffee) from Central and South America. Bananas Foster, a New Orleans original, was invented in 1951 by chef Paul Blangé at Brennan's. Named after owner Owen Edward Brennan's friend Richard Foster, it's totally decadent and usually served over vanilla ice cream—for brunch. I love bananas Foster stuffed into crêpes (see p. 20).

Éclairs

(Say it: EEE-claires)

My grandfather on my dad's side was a true character. He had this mint baby-blue ragtop convertible that he outfitted with this crazy musical horn that spewed outrageously loud and obnoxious tunes whenever he leaned on it. He loved nothing more than to coast into our driveway early on Sunday morning and lean on that horn, the tunes no doubt waking up any neighbor within earshot. I'd always try to dash out the door before my mom could, but most of the time she beat me to it, shooting out the door with daggers coming out of her eyes and screaming at Grandfather in her nightgown. My grandfather egged her on, changing the car horn's tune while she hollered, until I raced out the door and hopped in, which immediately put an end to the hullabaloo.

We'd cruise to McKenzie's, which was the bakery of New Orleans, and pick up glazed donuts or cinnamon buns to bring home, which always smoothed over any grudge my mom held. Grandfather let me pick out whatever sweet I wanted and I always chose the same thing— a shiny, chocolate-covered vanilla cream–filled éclair. The éclair never made it home because I devoured the whole delicious deal on the drive back. When I scooched out of the car, I'd leave a chocolate trail of glaze behind me stretching across Grandfather's white pleather seat. He didn't mind—in his eyes, I could do no wrong.

Éclairs

FOR THE PASTRY CREAM

5   large egg yolks

½   cup sugar

¼   cup cornstarch

2   cups whole milk

2   teaspoons vanilla extract

2   tablespoons unsalted butter

FOR THE PÂTE À CHOUX

4   tablespoons unsalted butter

1   tablespoon sugar

⅛   teaspoon salt

1   cup all-purpose flour

4-5 large eggs

FOR THE CHOCOLATE GLAZE

4   ounces bittersweet chocolate
     (preferably 66%–72% cacao),
     finely chopped

2   tablespoons light corn syrup

½   cup plus 2 tablespoons heavy
     cream

TO MAKE THE PASTRY CREAM

Beat the eggs, sugar, and cornstarch in a large bowl until smooth. Bring the milk to a boil in a medium saucepan over medium-high heat. Turn off the heat and, while whisking, slowly pour a little hot milk into the egg mixture. Once the eggs loosen up, drizzle in the rest of the milk, whisking constantly. Return the mixture to the saucepan and cook over low heat, whisking constantly, until it forms slow bubbles and is the consistency of thick pudding, about 1 minute. Turn off the heat, strain the mixture through a fine-mesh sieve into a medium bowl. Whisk in the vanilla and butter. Place a piece of plastic wrap on the surface of the pastry cream and refrigerate for at least 6 hours, or preferably overnight (the cream will keep for up to 3 days).

TO MAKE THE CHOUX

Heat the oven to 450°F and line a rimmed baking sheet with parchment. Place the butter, sugar, salt, and 1 cup of water in a small saucepan and bring to a simmer over medium heat. Reduce the heat to medium-low and stir in the flour with a wooden spoon. Continue to stir the mixture (aggressively toward the end as the dough forms a firmer ball) until the batter comes together in a loose ball. Continue to cook while stirring until the choux paste has a wheaty color and a sheen, 2½ to 3 minutes (the paste gets really stiff, so use those muscles!). Turn the hot dough out into the bowl of a stand mixer (or into a large bowl if using a hand mixer) and beat on medium speed for 20 seconds to let some of the heat out. Add the eggs, one at a time, beating for 30 seconds between additions to allow the egg to be completely incorporated into the batter before adding the next one. Scrape down the bottom and sides of the bowl as necessary. After you add 4 eggs, check the consistency of the paste. If it has a sheen and falls from the paddle in long gluey strands, you're done. If it's still a little thick and clumpy, beat in the remaining egg.

Using a rubber spatula, scrape the batter into a gallon-size resealable plastic bag and cut a ½-inch hole in one of the corners (or use a piping bag fitted with a 1-inch tip). Pipe twelve 4-inch-long by 2-inch-wide strips on the prepared baking sheet and bake until the shells are golden on the sides and golden-brown on top and have nearly tripled in size, about 15 minutes. Rotate the sheet pan, reduce the oven temperature to 350°F, and continue to bake until uniformly brown, about 25 minutes. Turn the oven off and remove the pan from the oven. Holding the éclair shell with a kitchen towel and using a paring knife, poke a small hole in each end, twisting the knife to make a slightly larger opening before pulling the knife out. Place the baking sheet back in the oven (even though it is off, it will still be warm inside) to let the pastry dry out for 15 minutes. Remove from the oven and cool completely on a rack. (If you're not planning on filling the éclair shells within a few hours, store in an airtight container for up to 24 hours.)

TIP Add 2 tablespoons of heavy cream to the leftover glaze for a killer sauce to go with Straight Up Vanilla Bean Ice Cream (p. 110).

While the choux pastry cools, make the chocolate glaze: Place the chocolate and corn syrup in a small bowl. Bring the cream to a boil in a small saucepan over medium-high heat. Pour over the chocolate, cover with plastic wrap, and let the mixture sit for 1 minute. Using a whisk, begin to gently stir the mixture in the center of the bowl until it begins to come together, then work in the rest of the cream from the edges of the bowl, whisking slowly so you don't get air bubbles. The chocolate glaze will be very smooth and shiny. (The glaze can be made up to 2 days in advance and stored, covered with plastic wrap, in the refrigerator. Microwave for 30 seconds and stir until slightly soft and smooth before using.)

When you're ready to serve, fill a pastry bag fitted with a 7-mm tip with the pastry cream. Insert the tip into one of the holes you created in the bottom of the éclair shells and squeeze some pastry cream into the shell (just enough so it feels heavy—if you fill it too full, the pastry cream will bust out the sides). Remove the tip and repeat with the other hole. Hold the éclair upside down and dip it into the glaze, then set it on a cooling rack to dry. Repeat filling and glazing the remaining shells. Éclairs are best eaten within 15 or 20 minutes of glazing, so the glaze is set and the shell is still crisp. They can be refrigerated for up to 2 hours, but note that the shell will soften slightly.

MAKES 10 ÉCLAIRS

ODE TO McKENZIE'S

cKenzie's Pastry Shoppe was a New Orleans institution with 40-plus stores in the area. Though it was beloved by many (myself included) for its sticky-sweet cinnamon buns, king cakes, chocolate-covered turtles, and glazed buttermilk drop donuts, the franchise succumbed to debt at the turn of the millennium. People used to say that you couldn't throw a stone in the city without hitting a McKenzie's. How I wish that saying were still true.

Double Chocolate Bread Pudding
with Salted Bourbon Caramel Sauce

Every year for Christmas, my mom and dad pulled out all the stops and took the family to Galatoire's on Bourbon Street, one of the few places in New Orleans where a jacket is still required for the gentlemen. Galatoire's for Christmas Eve or Christmas Day dinner is no joke—not even Tennessee Williams could reserve a table in advance. We'd bribe someone to save our spot in line, and he or she would wait there for sometimes up to eight hours to score us a table. The men and women who crowded the parlor-like dining room were decked out with so many bobbles and flashing lights attached to their sweaters, ears, and even on top of their heads that they looked like lit-up Christmas trees. At the end of the meal, after every drop of béarnaise sauce had been mopped off our plates, out would come Galatoire's famous banana bread pudding, made with lots of cinnamon and nutmeg and served with a whiskey raisin sauce.

Bread pudding is one of my favorite holiday traditions, and I make it for my family every holiday season. It's great for large gatherings and potlucks because it can be made up to three days ahead of time. This chocolate version is amazing when served with salted bourbon caramel. In New Orleans you'd make bread pudding with airy Leidenheimer French bread, but I find that brioche, challah, or even day-old croissants or king cake make for an outrageously decadent pudding (just don't tell your momma it ain't Leidenheimer!).

Double Chocolate Bread Pudding

2 tablespoons unsalted butter, at room temperature

1 pound brioche bread, crust removed and sliced into 1-inch cubes

6 large eggs

1/3 cup Dutch-processed cocoa powder

12 ounces bittersweet chocolate (preferably 66%–72% cacao), finely chopped

5½ cups whole milk

2½ cups heavy cream

1¾ cups sugar

¼ teaspoon salt

¾ teaspoon vanilla extract

FOR THE CARAMEL SAUCE

1½ cups sugar

¾ cup heavy cream

2 tablespoons unsalted butter, at room temperature

¼ cup bourbon

¼ teaspoon salt

TO MAKE THE PUDDING

Heat the oven to 325°F. Grease a 13x9-inch baking dish with the softened butter and set aside.

Place the bread cubes on a rimmed baking sheet and toast in the oven until golden-brown, 12 to 15 minutes, rotating midway through. Set aside to cool.

Place the bread in the prepared baking dish and set aside. Whisk the eggs in a medium bowl and set aside. Sift the cocoa into a medium bowl and set aside.

Place the chocolate in a large bowl. Bring the milk, cream, sugar, and salt to a boil in a large pot, stirring occasionally to dissolve the sugar. Turn off the heat, stir in the vanilla, and then pour the hot mixture over the chopped chocolate. Cover the bowl with plastic wrap, set aside for 5 minutes, and then whisk until smooth.

Whisk ½ cup of the chocolate mixture into the cocoa, stirring until smooth. Whisk in another ½ cup of the chocolate mixture and then whisk in the eggs. Transfer to the large bowl of remaining chocolate mixture and whisk until they are completely incorporated.

Pour all but 1 cup of the chocolate mixture over the bread cubes in the baking dish and set aside so the bread can soak up the liquid. Press down on the bread with a wooden spoon every 15 minutes for 1 hour, adding the rest of the chocolate mixture after about 30 minutes, or when the bread has soaked up enough so the last cup of liquid will fit.

Heat the oven to 350°F.

Cover the bread pudding with aluminum foil and use a paring knife to make 4 small slits in the foil to allow steam to escape. Set the baking dish in a large roasting pan and place in the oven. Pour enough hot water in the roasting pan so the water reaches 1 inch up the side of the baking dish (if you don't have a roasting pan large enough to fit the baking dish, set the dish onto a rimmed baking sheet and slide it in the oven, adding enough water to the baking sheet so it cushions the baking dish but doesn't spill over). Bake for 45 minutes, and then remove the foil and bake until the pudding begins to puff slightly and the center bounces back to light pressure, about another 25 to 35 minutes. Cool for 30 minutes.

TO MAKE THE SAUCE

While the bread pudding cools, make the caramel. Place the sugar in a 2-quart saucepan and add ¼ cup of water. Cover (or if you can't find a lid, top the sauce-pan with a heatproof bowl, making sure the bottom of the bowl doesn't touch the sugar) and cook over medium heat, swirling the mixture every 1 to 2 minutes, until the sugar is liquefied, about 6 minutes. Continue to cook until the sugar is a medium-amber color, another 4 to 6 minutes. Turn off the heat and add the cream (it will vigorously bubble up at first), whisking the mixture until smooth, then add the softened butter, bourbon, and salt. Set aside and serve with the still-warm bread pudding.

SERVES 10 TO 12

→MAKE AHEAD Bread pudding is one of those desserts that is great for entertaining because it can be made and refrigerated a few days ahead of time. To warm, reheat the entire pan of bread pudding in a water bath in a 350°F oven until the center is warm. Or, for individual portions, slice and reheat in your microwave or toaster oven. The caramel can be covered and stored at room temperature for 2 days, or covered and refrigerated for up to 2 weeks ahead of time. Reheat the sauce in a saucepan or in your microwave.

LEIDENHEIMER BREAD

For more than a century, the G. H. Leidenheimer Baking Company has baked up New Orleans' signature French bread—crisp and crackly on the outside and pillowy-tender within. Many New Orleanians say that the bread is the secret ingredient to the best po' boys at Domilise's or Mother's. I would have to agree.

German immigrant George Leidenheimer opened the bakery in 1896, and just a couple of years later, he moved it to where it stands today on Simon Bolivar Avenue. It's still family owned and operated by fourth-generation Leidenheimers, my dear friend, Katherine, and her brother, Sandy Whann. The bakery is known for its baguettes, mini-size petite pistolettes, and bread for muffulettas, that massive round sandwich popularized at the Central Grocery on Decatur.

After Hurricane Katrina, the bakery shut down due to lack of electricity and bakers (who had fled the city). Until the bakery was operational again, a Leidenheimer baker kneaded and baked bread in Chicago so clients across the country wouldn't have to go without their French bread. In 2005 the Leidenheimer Baking Company was the recipient of the Guardian of Tradition award from the Southern Foodways Alliance.

Crêpes du Vieux Carré

(Say it: crehps de view car-A)

⊰⊱⊰⊱⊰⊱⊰⊱⊰⊱⊰⊱⊰⊱⊰⊱⊰⊱⊰⊱⊰⊱⊰⊱⊰⊱⊰⊱

Though the concept of crêpes is a holdover from way back when the French called Louisiana their territory, you can be sure that New Orleanians have turned them into their own deal, stuffing them with seafood and loading 'em down with 20 pounds of cheese!

Once I got into the pastry business, I realized that there were about as many recipes for crêpes as there were people making them. My recipe is super simple and doesn't require any special trickery or difficult technique aside from flipping the crêpe. I give you my way of flipping in the recipe, but I'm sure that after making the first few crêpes (and don't worry, even I throw away the first couple) you'll develop your own method.

You can cook the crêpes right away after making the batter, or for extra-tender crêpes, make the batter the night before and cook the crêpes for breakfast the following morning (the batter keeps for a couple of days). Fold them into quarters with granulated sugar and a pad of butter, top with confectioners' sugar, or for a sweeter take, serve stuffed with bananas Foster (p. 10), with the macerated strawberries from the strawberry shortcake recipe on p. 70, or with blueberry jam (p. 122) or strawberry jam (p. 125). If you don't have an 11-inch nonstick skillet, you can use a 10- or 12-inch nonstick pan and decrease or increase the amount of batter accordingly.

⊰⊱⊰⊱⊰⊱⊰⊱⊰⊱⊰⊱⊰⊱⊰⊱⊰⊱⊰⊱⊰⊱⊰⊱⊰⊱⊰⊱

6 tablespoons unsalted butter

1¾ cups whole milk

3 large eggs

3 large egg yolks

1 cup all-purpose flour

¼ cup sugar

½ teaspoon salt

1 tablespoon brandy or dark rum (optional)

Confectioners' sugar or jam for serving

Place the butter in a 2-cup liquid measuring cup and microwave in 20-second increments until melted. Add the milk and microwave in 20-second increments until it's warm to the touch. Whisk together and pour into a large bowl. Whisk the eggs and egg yolks together in a medium bowl and set aside.

Place the flour, sugar, and salt in a fine-mesh sieve and sift half of it into the butter-milk mixture. Whisk to combine, and then whisk in the eggs in 4 additions, mixing until just incorporated before adding the next. Add the liquor (if using) and then sift in the remaining dry ingredients, whisking until combined. Strain the batter through a sieve into a clean bowl. Cover with plastic wrap and refrigerate overnight, or use immediately.

To make the crêpes, place a folded kitchen towel next to your cooking surface. Spray a medium nonstick skillet with nonstick cooking spray and place over medium-low heat for 2 minutes.

Using a measuring cup or a small ladle, pour ¼ cup of batter (if using an 11-inch skillet; if using a smaller skillet, pour in less batter) into the pan and swirl it around to evenly coat the pan bottom, trying not to get the batter too far up the pan sides. Cook the crêpe until the edges begin to brown, 1½ to 2 minutes, shaking the pan occasionally to release the crêpe from the bottom of the pan.

Remove the pan from the heat and tilt it away from you. Give the pan a few taps on the towel to slide the crêpe halfway out of the skillet. Flip the crêpe with a quick flick of your wrist, using your fingers to quickly move the crêpe back into place. Cook until the second side is set, about 1 minute, and slide it out of the pan and onto a plate. Serve with confectioners' sugar, roll with jam, or stuff with bananas Foster or strawberry sauce.

MAKES 16 CRÊPES

King Cake

❧❧❧❧❧❧❧❧❧❧❧❧❧❧❧❧❧❧❧❧❧❧

January 6, also known as Twelfth Night, marks the beginning of New Orleans' Carnival celebrations and the start of king cake season. King cake is to Mardi Gras what pumpkin pie is to Thanksgiving—the holiday just wouldn't be the same without it. Every table in every home, office, cafeteria, and lounge will be graced by a king cake at some point between Twelfth Night and Fat Tuesday, when Lent begins. During this time, which can happily stretch for months depending on the calendar year, New Orleans is invaded by king cakes and king cake parties.

Similar to a glazed coffee cake, king cake is more of a sweet bread than a cake, laced with cinnamon, shaped like a braid or a crown (depending on the baker), and decorated with sugar tinted the three colors of Mardi Gras: gold for power, green for faith, and purple for justice. As a bonus, a tiny plastic baby (or a coin or dried bean) is hidden in the cake; whoever gets the piece with the prize gets to host the next king cake party and supply the king cake. So while most parts of the country spend January, February, and March recovering from the decadence of the holidays, New Orleanians are once again eating, celebrating, and living life to the max.

When I was in high school, some friends and I would stop at McKenzie's bakery on the way to swim team practice, buy a king cake, and try to out-eat one another while driving to the pool. Whoever finished the king cake by the time we got to practice was the winner and undisputed master of the king cake—needless to say we weren't the speediest (or most buoyant) swimmers during Carnival season!

❧❧❧❧❧❧❧❧❧❧❧❧❧❧❧❧❧❧❧❧❧❧

King Cake

FOR THE CAKE

1   (1¼-ounce) package dry-active yeast

¼   cup warm milk (105°F–115°F or warm to the touch)

1   cup plus 6 tablespoons bread flour plus extra for rolling

1   tablespoon honey

¾   cup cake flour

2   large eggs

1   large egg yolk

2   tablespoons sugar

½   teaspoon ground cinnamon

½   teaspoon vanilla extract

¼   teaspoon almond extract

1   teaspoon salt

5   tablespoons unsalted butter, at room temperature

1   plastic baby figurine (to hide in the cake), optional

FOR THE EGG WASH

1   large egg

1   tablespoon milk

FOR THE ICING AND DECORATION

2   cups confectioners' sugar, sifted

2   tablespoons light corn syrup

3   tablespoons milk

¼   teaspoon vanilla extract

3   cups sugar

    Green food coloring

    Gold or yellow food coloring

    Purple or red and blue food coloring

TO MAKE THE CAKE

Whisk the yeast with the warm milk in the bowl of a stand mixer until dissolved. Add the 6 tablespoons of bread flour and the honey and, using the paddle attachment, mix on low speed until fairly smooth (there will still be a few lumps), 30 seconds to 1 minute, scraping the bottom and sides of the bowl as necessary. Cover with plastic wrap and let rise until doubled in volume, about 20 minutes.

Once the dough has doubled, add ¾ cup of the remaining bread flour, the cake flour, eggs, egg yolk, sugar, cinnamon, vanilla and almond extracts, and salt. Mix on low speed until combined, then switch to a dough hook, increase the speed to medium, and beat until smooth, about 2 minutes. Increase the speed to medium-high and begin adding 4 tablespoons of the butter 1 tablespoon at a time, mixing well between additions. Continue to knead until the dough forms a slack ball (it will ride the dough hook, be tacky, and not slap the bottom of the bowl, but it should generally come together into a loose mass), 2 to 3 minutes. If the dough doesn't come together, continue kneading while adding up to ¼ cup of the reserved bread flour, until it does.

Grease a large bowl with ½ tablespoon of the remaining butter and transfer the dough to the bowl, turning it over in the bowl to coat with butter. Cover the bowl with a piece of plastic wrap or damp kitchen towel and place the bowl in a draft-free spot until the dough has doubled in size, about 1 hour.

Line a rimmed baking sheet with parchment paper and grease the parchment paper with the remaining butter. Generously flour your work surface using the remaining ¼ cup of bread flour (if you used the bread flour in the dough, dust your work surface with more bread flour). Turn the dough out onto the work surface and sprinkle the top with some flour. Use your hands to press and flatten it into a rectangle. Using a rolling pin, roll the dough into a ¼-inch-thick strip that is about 24 inches long by about 6 inches wide. Starting with one of the long sides, roll the dough on top of itself, making a long, thin baguette-shaped length. Pinch the edge to the body of the dough to seal, turn the dough so it lies horizontally on your work surface, and gently roll it on your work surface to even out any bulges and create a somewhat consistent 1½-inch-wide rope. Bring the two ends of the dough together and pinch them into one another to seal. Carefully transfer the dough oval or circle to the prepared sheet pan. Cover with a piece of plastic wrap or a damp kitchen towel and set in a warm, dry spot to rise until doubled, about 1 hour.

Heat the oven to 375°F. To make the egg wash, whisk the egg and the milk together in a small bowl. Brush the egg wash over the top and sides of the dough, and bake the king cake until golden and cooked through, 25 to 30 minutes. Immediately after removing the cake from the oven, make a small slit in the bottom of the cake and insert the baby figurine (if using). Set on a rack to cool completely.

TO MAKE THE ICING

While the cake cools, make the icing. Whisk the confectioners' sugar, corn syrup, milk, and vanilla together in the bowl of a stand mixer on low speed until smooth and completely incorporated. Cover the bowl with a damp kitchen towel until you are ready to glaze the cake.

To make the colored sugar, measure 1 cup of the sugar into each of 3 resealable quart-size plastic bags. Add 4 drops of green food coloring to one bag, 4 drops of gold or yellow food coloring to another bag, and 4 drops of purple food coloring to the last bag (if you don't have purple, make it yourself: measure 2 drops of red and 2 drops of blue food coloring onto a spoon and mix with a cake tester or toothpick until combined). Seal each bag and then vigorously shake to combine the sugar and food coloring.

Spoon the icing over the cooled cake. Immediately after icing, decorate with the tinted sugar. I like to alternate colors every 2½ inches, but you can also divide the cake into 3 sections and apply one color to each section. Slice and serve immediately or store in a cake box or on a baking sheet placed within a large plastic bag (unscented trash bags work well) for up to 2 days.

MAKES 1 CAKE

Calas Fried Rice Fritters

(Say it: cahl-LAHSS)

❧❧❧❧❧❧❧❧❧❧❧❧❧❧❧❧❧❧❧❧

This is a recipe lost to most New Orleanians, save for a few old bucks and grannys who can remember calas fried rice fritters being sold in the streets first thing in the morning in the French Quarter by women of African descent who carried them in baskets balanced on their heads, shouting out "Belle cala! Tout chaud!" Crisp around the edges with a plump, toothsome belly, these fritters beg to be served with obscene quantities of earthy, sorghum-like cane syrup, though traditionalists may opt for confectioners' sugar instead. A cup of strong coffee or a café au lait is the ideal accompaniment.

While old-school recipes call for cooking rice until it's mushy and then letting it rise with yeast overnight, I like my fritters with distinct grains of rice suspended in a light batter that's leavened with baking powder rather than yeast. It's important to make the fritters with cold rice so the grains remain separate and don't clump together in the fritter batter. See p. 165 for cane syrup ordering sources, or substitute sorghum or maple syrup instead (but you didn't hear that from me!).

❧❧❧❧❧❧❧❧❧❧❧❧❧❧❧❧❧❧❧❧

Calas Fried Rice Fritters

½ cup long-grain white rice (Mahatma® brand if you can find it)

Peanut oil for frying

1 cup all-purpose flour

1 teaspoon baking powder

½ teaspoon ground cinnamon

3 large eggs

2 tablespoons sugar

1 teaspoon vanilla extract

½ teaspoon salt

Cane syrup for serving

→TIP I usually make calas when I have leftover rice in the fridge—whether it's from Monday's red beans or Chinese takeout. If using leftover rice, add 1½ cups of cooked, cold rice to the batter.

Bring 1 cup of water and a pinch of salt to a boil in a small saucepan. Add the rice, stir once, reduce the heat to low, and cover the pan, cooking 18 to 20 minutes or until the grains of rice are plump and fluff apart with a fork. Turn the rice out onto a parchment paper–lined baking sheet and cool for 15 minutes, then transfer to a plastic container (don't pack it in). Cover with plastic wrap and poke a few holes in the top. Refrigerate for at least 8 hours or up to 2 days.

Pour enough peanut oil into a large pot to fill it to a 2½- to 3-inch depth and bring to a temperature between 350°F and 360°F over medium heat (see "How to Fry" on the facing page). Line a plate with paper towels and set aside.

While the oil heats up, place the flour, baking powder, and cinnamon in a medium bowl. Using a stand mixer or a hand mixer, beat the eggs, sugar, and vanilla on high speed until foamy and tripled in volume, 1½ to 2 minutes. Sift in half of the dry ingredients, add the salt, and mix on low speed until only a few dry streaks remain. Sift in the remaining dry ingredients and mix on low speed for a few turns, then add the rice and mix until the fritter batter just comes together into a loose, roughly textured ball.

Once your oil is hot, dip a teaspoon in the hot oil, then into the batter and scoop out a heaping teaspoonful. Hold the spoon close to the oil and let the batter roll off and into the oil. Repeat with the remaining batter; using a slotted spoon, turn and baste the fritters occasionally, allowing them to become golden brown on all sides. (Fry the fritters in two batches if your pot becomes overcrowded.) If the temperature of the oil dips below 350°F, increase the heat to medium-high. Once the fritters are golden brown, transfer them to the prepared plate to cool slightly. Serve on a small plate drizzled with lots of cane syrup.

MAKES 3 TO 3½ DOZEN

How to Fry

I always begin to heat my oil about 30 minutes before I'm going to need to fry whatever I am making, be it beignets, calas, or fried chicken. Bringing the oil up to temperature nice and slow makes it easier to avoid overheating the oil, which can cause it to smoke and lend a bitter flavor to the food you cook (even if you catch the spike in temp in time and lower the heat accordingly).

Once you add your fritters (or whatever) to the pot, watch the temperature on a thermometer—if you add too many items at once, the temperature can dip, in which case you'd want to turn up the heat to bring the oil back up to where you want it to be. When you fry food in colder oil (less than 350°F), the food absorbs oil and becomes greasy. Frying in hot oil, say 350°F to 375°F, cooks the outer layer of the food quickly, creating a shield against oil absorption. That's why it's important to be patient and make sure your oil is hot (but not too hot!) before frying. It can mean the difference between a crisp calas and a soggy one.

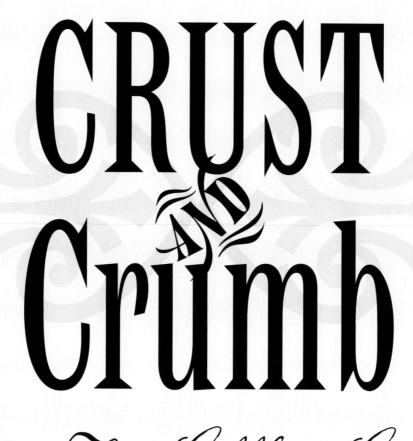

CRUST AND Crumb

Pies, Tarts, Cobblers & Crisps

❧❦❧❦❧❦❧❦❧❦❧❦❧❦❧❦❧❦❧❦❧❦❧❦❧❦

As comforting as your favorite T-shirt and as easy as worn-in blue jeans, these recipes are the ones that I turn to all the time for a dessert to serve to company or just to have around. From my Great Aunt Patty's (aka "The GAP") fried apple pies to Nana's Banana Bread and a Lemon Icebox Pie inspired by the stellar version at Clancy's restaurant, these are the sweet endings that bring me back home every time.

❧❦❧❦❧❦❧❦❧❦❧❦❧❦❧❦❧❦❧❦❧❦❧❦❧❦

The GAP's Fried Apple Pie

Living in New Orleans, I knew when summer was coming to an end not when my mom took me to get fitted for my new Catholic school uniform but when my Great Aunt Patty (aka "The GAP") from Tennessee pulled into my driveway in her little Honda® Civic for her annual visit. Anticipating her arrival, my sister and I would wait for her to show up all day long, knowing that the sooner she showed, the quicker our favorite apple pie would be coming out of the oven. We were always well prepared for her visit, making sure that everything she'd need to make the pie was neatly placed on the counter—the apples in a bowl, the whole nutmeg out with the grater on the side, the cornstarch, the sugar, the butter, and a six-pack of Coca Cola® (her beverage of choice for six decades; she even kept a glass of the stuff at her bedside instead of water), chilled and ready to drink. No sooner than she walked in the door did we put her to work. She humored us, and I thank her for that, as well as for her amazing apple pie.

I've adapted The GAP's pie to suit my grown-up taste by paying tribute to my Latin American heritage while also giving props to my favorite childhood brown bag treat, Hubig's fried pies (see p. 36). The result is these cute, mini fried apple pies that can be eaten out of hand, like empanadas. The second way that I changed her recipe is by adding ground cinnamon to the filling. This is sacrilege to The GAP, who never, ever used anything but fresh-grated whole nutmeg in her pie. I hope she can forgive me.

The GAP's Fried Apple Pie

FOR THE DOUGH

4	cups all-purpose flour plus more for rolling
1½	teaspoons baking powder
¾	teaspoon salt
½	cup (8 tablespoons) vegetable shortening, melted and cooled
2	large eggs
¾	cup whole milk

FOR THE FILLING

½	cup apple cider or apple juice
1	tablespoon cornstarch
5	firm, juicy apples (preferably Braeburn), peeled, cored, and diced into ¼-inch cubes
½	cup sugar
½	teaspoon ground nutmeg (preferably freshly ground)
¼	teaspoon ground cinnamon
1	vanilla bean, halved widthwise
1	tablespoon unsalted butter

Peanut oil for frying

Confectioners' sugar for serving

TO MAKE THE DOUGH

Sift the flour, baking powder, and salt into the bowl of a stand mixer (use a large bowl if mixing by hand). Add the melted shortening, eggs, and milk. Using the paddle attachment, mix the dough on low speed until the dry ingredients are moistened. Increase the speed to medium and knead the dough until it is no longer sticky, about 2 to 3 minutes, adding more flour, 1 tablespoon at a time, if the dough seems very wet or sticky. (If mixing by hand, it will take about 5 minutes to knead the dough.) Divide the dough in half, wrap each half in plastic wrap, and refrigerate for 1 hour (because the dough turns gray, it is best used within 6 hours of making; see "Make Ahead" on the facing page for freezing instructions).

TO MAKE THE FILLING

Meanwhile, make the apple filling. Line a rimmed baking sheet with parchment paper. Whisk ¼ cup of the apple juice or cider with the cornstarch in a small bowl and set aside. Place the apples, sugar, nutmeg, and cinnamon in a large bowl. Wrap one-half of the vanilla bean well in plastic wrap, and reserve for another use. Slice the remaining half lengthwise down the middle. Open the pod and use the knife to scrape out the seeds; discard the pod. Add the seeds to the apples and toss with the sugar and spices.

Melt the butter in a large pot over medium-high heat. Once melted, let the butter simmer for 20 seconds, then stir in the apples. Cook with a lid askew until the apples start to soften, about 5 to 7 minutes, stirring occasionally. Add the remaining ¼ cup of apple juice or cider and simmer, stirring occasionally, until the liquid is reduced by half, about 2 to 3 minutes. Stir in the cornstarch slurry and cook until the mixture is thickened, 3 to 4 minutes. Transfer to the prepared baking sheet (or a large bowl) and cool to room temperature, and then cover with plastic wrap and refrigerate until cold.

TO MAKE THE PIECRUSTS

Once the apples have chilled, make the piecrusts. Line a rimmed baking sheet with parchment paper. Place a small dish of water next to your work surface. Generously flour the work surface and roll one dough ball into a ⅛-inch-thick circle. Use a 3½- to 4-inch biscuit or cookie cutter to cut out rounds from the dough. Place the circles on the prepared baking sheet, cover with a sheet of parchment paper and place them in the refrigerator to keep cool. Set the dough scraps aside and reflour your work surface. Repeat with the second piece of dough and refrigerate the stamped-out rounds. Press all of the scraps together, roll them into a ⅛-inch-thick circle, cut out rounds, and refrigerate. Discard the leftover scraps. (Discard the scraps after rolling the second time; the dough gets too tough to roll a third time.)

→**TIME SAVER** When I'm craving The GAP's fried pies but don't have time to make my own dough, I use prepared empanada dough from the frozen foods section of my local Latin supermarket (make sure you buy the one made specifically for frying and not for baking). It fries up beautifully and tastes almost as good!

TO ASSEMBLE THE PIES

Place 1½ to 2 tablespoons of cold apple filling in the center of each dough circle. Using your finger or a pastry brush, moisten the edge of the bottom half of the circle with water and fold the top half over, bringing the edges together and pressing them tightly to seal. Using firm pressure, crimp the edges of the dough using an upturned fork. Refrigerate the filled pies while you heat the oil. (The pies can be made up to 6 hours before frying.)

Line a plate with paper towels. Pour enough peanut oil into a large pot to fill it to a 3-inch depth and bring to a temperature of 375°F over high heat. Fry a few turnovers (you don't want to fry too many at one time, otherwise the temperature of the oil will drop and the turnovers will become greasy) until all sides are golden brown, about 3 to 5 minutes, turning them over often. Transfer to the prepared plate to drain while you fry the remaining turnovers. Serve warm or at room temperature with plenty of confectioners' sugar on top.

MAKES 18 MINI PIES

→**MAKE AHEAD** The apple filling can be made up to 2 days ahead, and the stamped-out dough circles can be frozen for up to 6 months. Freeze the dough circles flat on the parchment paper–lined baking sheet (if you need to stack the dough, separate the layers with parchment paper). Once frozen solid, transfer the circles to a resealable freezer bag. To use, return the circles to a parchment paper–lined baking sheet, cover them with another sheet, defrost in your refrigerator overnight, and then fill. The filled and crimped pies can be refrigerated for up to 6 hours before frying.

HUBIG'S PIES
(Say it: HYOU-bigs)

In the Faubourg Marigny (say it: FAW-burg marin-knee) neighborhood on Dauphine Street is the Simon Hubig Pie Company, a bakery that produces some 30,000 hand-size pies a day. Made with a from-scratch piecrust and filled with seasonal and mostly local fruit like cherries, peaches, sweet potatoes, lemon, and apple, they're a beloved staple of school kids, truck drivers, and legislators alike—heck, even long-term overnighters at the Orleans Parish Jail are fans.

Simon Hubig, a German immigrant, opened the first Hubig's in Fort Worth, Texas, around the time of World War I. A few years later, he had locations in several cities, including New Orleans. Aspirations of a national chain were stomped on after the stock market crash took its toll. The New Orleans location, opened in 1922, is the only one still operating today. After Katrina, the bakery lost a few trucks and about half its employees. It shut down for a few months—when it reopened the city rejoiced that "Savory Simon," the Hubig's chef mascot on the front of the package, was back. Whenever I'm in New Orleans, one of the first things I do is to stop at a convenience store or pharmacy to pick up a Hubig's pie. It always tastes just like home.

Pecan Pie

(Say it: peh-CAHN)

I've probably been eating pecan pie since I was in diapers. Nut allergies? Please. Southerners are weaned from the bottle with pecan pie, celebrate marriage with pecan pie, and say goodbye to their loved ones with pecan pie. When I was in my teens, I'd go to the Camellia Grill on Carrollton Avenue and sit at the counter for a burger, dressed (in New Orleans-ese that means with lettuce, tomatoes, and mayo), cheese fries, and pecan pie, grilled on the flat top on both sides and then topped with a scoop of vanilla ice cream.

That said, like most Louisianans, I ate the bulk of my pecan pie at the kitchen table surrounded by relatives and relations. I'm particularly loyal to Louisiana-grown ingredients, which is why in addition to Louisiana pecans (see p. 39) I like to sweeten pecan pie with cane syrup rather than corn syrup or molasses. Cane syrup gives this pie the earthiness of molasses minus its bitter qualities and is a whole lot more interesting, flavor-wise, than corn syrup. While I still have a soft spot for vanilla ice cream (see p. 110), the Pecan & Brown Butter Ice Cream on p. 116 makes a killer topping.

Pecan Pie

FOR THE CRUST

- 1½ cups all-purpose flour plus extra for rolling
- 2 tablespoons sugar
- ½ teaspoon salt
- 1½ sticks (12 tablespoons) unsalted butter, cut into small cubes
- 5–7 tablespoons ice water

FOR THE FILLING

- 1 large egg
- 5 large egg yolks
- ⅔ cup Steen's™ cane syrup
- ⅔ cup light brown sugar
- ½ cup heavy cream
- ¼ teaspoon salt
- 1 stick unsalted butter, cut into small pieces
- 1 teaspoon vanilla extract
- 1½ cups pecan pieces

TO MAKE THE CRUST

Pulse the flour, sugar, and salt together in the bowl of a food processor until combined. Add the butter and pulse until the smallest pieces are about the size of corn kernels, 10 to 12 pulses. Add 5 tablespoons of water and pulse until the dough is no longer dry (when squeezed in your hand, it should form a ball and hold its shape), 4 to 6 times (if the dough is still dry, add another tablespoon or two of ice water). Turn the dough out onto your work surface and form it into a disk. Wrap the dough in plastic wrap and chill for at least 1 hour or up to 3 days (or freeze for up to 1 month; defrost in the refrigerator overnight before using).

Heat the oven to 325°F. Remove the dough from the refrigerator (let it sit out at room temperature for 5 minutes to soften). Flour your work surface and roll the dough into a 12-inch circle, ⅛ inch thick. Fold the dough into quarters and transfer to a 9½-inch pie plate. Unfold the dough and fit it into the pie plate, then trim off all but ¼ inch of the overhang. Using your thumb and index finger, pinch the edge of the dough together to form a granny crimp. Chill while you make the filling.

TO MAKE THE FILLING

Whisk the egg and the egg yolks together in a large bowl and set aside. Combine the cane syrup, sugar, cream, and salt in a medium saucepan. Add the butter and melt over medium heat. Once the butter has melted, continue to cook the mixture until it is hot but not bubbling, about 1 minute. Whisk the sugar mixture into the egg yolks a little at a time, just until the bottom of the bowl is warm to the touch, and then add the remaining sugar mixture. Stir in the vanilla and set aside.

Take the pie plate out of the refrigerator. Sprinkle the pecan pieces into the piecrust and pour the filling on top. Bake until the center has a little resistance, like a soft-setting custard, 30 to 40 minutes. Remove from the oven and cool for at least 1 hour before slicing and serving.

MAKES ONE 9½-INCH PIE

VARIATION

BOURBON-CHOCOLATE CHIP PECAN PIE

Follow the recipe, but add 2 tablespoons of bourbon along with the vanilla to the hot egg-sugar base. Transfer the mixture to a large bowl and place it in an ice-water bath to chill for 8 minutes, stirring occasionally. Place 1¼ cups of pecans into the pie shell and top with an even layer of ½ cup of semisweet chocolate chips (or roughly chopped semisweet chocolate). Pour the slightly cooled filling into the shell and bake according to the recipe.

LOUISIANA PECANS

Granny and I used to comb the neutral grounds (called medians in the rest of the country) across from my dad's veterinary clinic on Elysian Fields looking for fallen pecans. We'd load up our Schwegmann's plastic bags with the nuts and bring them home to shell and bake with. I'm still convinced that Louisiana-grown pecans are like no other—must be the humidity or maybe because we're below sea level. All I know is that they're just so good, and I can't imagine a holiday table without a bowl of them.

Louisiana has a long history with the pecan tree, a species of hickory that is native to North America. Derived from an Algonquian word meaning a nut that requires a stone to crack, fresh-shelled pecans are tender, buttery, rich, and sweet—a must-have for making iconic Louisianan sweets like pralines (p. 143), bananas Foster (p. 10), and of course pecan pie (see the facing page). According to the U.S. Department of Agriculture, the pecan is the most antioxidant-rich tree nut there is, so you can feel good about eating them, too. While Louisiana isn't the number one pecan producer in the United States, the state's ties to pecan growing are deep-seated. In fact, it was the distribution hub in New Orleans on the Mississippi River that launched pecan distribution to other parts of the country.

Pecan harvest begins in the fall (just in time for the holidays), with many Louisianans picking pecans that have fallen from trees in their yards. Unshelled, the nuts keep for about a year in a cool, dark, and dry spot. Shelled halves and pieces will keep for 9 months in the fridge or up to 2 years in the freezer.

Sweet Potato Tart Tatin

My Uncle Alfred, who wasn't an uncle but rather a good friend of my granny's, would put us kids to work whenever we visited his farm in Independence, Louisiana. While my parents, aunts, and uncles shelled pecans and drank bourbon or box wine at the picnic tables out back, my cousins would dig up sweet potatoes and pick green beans in the garden. I'd usually help out for a bit before Uncle Alfred commissioned me to hunt up a squirrel for dinner (he hated squirrels with a passion, and I loved to hunt, so we met each other's needs perfectly). We'd turn the squirrel into Cajun-style squirrel stew, wrap the sweet potatoes in aluminum foil jackets, and then roast them campfire-style over an open-pit fire. Sliced open and smothered with butter and brown sugar, extra-sweetened sweet potatoes remain one of my favorite foods today.

This tart tatin is an elegant but easy way to relive my love of sticky-sweet sweet potatoes in a more adult package. First, I make a super traditional French-style caramel sauce and pour it into a good ol' cast iron pan (passed down by Aunt Boo), a staple in Cajun kitchens. Then I layer thin slices of sweet potatoes on top (if you have a mandolin now is a great time to break that baby out of the box and use it to slice the sweet potatoes) and cover with puff pastry. After a little sojourn into the oven, the whole shebang comes out golden and gorgeous.

Sweet Potato Tart Tatin

1 sheet all-butter store-bought puff pastry, thawed

¾ cup sugar plus 1 tablespoon for pastry

1 stick unsalted butter, cut into 16 pieces

2 teaspoons vanilla extract

⅛ teaspoon salt

1½ pounds sweet potatoes (try to buy potatoes of relatively even width and few bulges), peeled, ends removed, and sliced into ⅛-inch-thick rounds

1 large egg

1 tablespoon milk

Ice cream for serving (optional)

Heat the oven to 375°F. Line a baking sheet with parchment paper. Place the puff pastry sheet on your work surface and cut out a 10-inch circle. Set the circle onto the prepared baking sheet. Prick the pastry all over with a fork and refrigerate.

Place ¾ cup of sugar in a small saucepan and cover with ¼ cup of water. Gently stir with a spoon to make sure all of the sugar is wet (it should have the consistency of wet sand), place a cover on slightly askew, and bring to a boil over medium-high heat. Keep the mixture covered until the syrup is clear and producing syrupy-looking medium-size bubbles, 3 to 4 minutes. Remove the cover and continue to cook until the sugar is a light butterscotch color and its temperature reaches 320°F. Turn off the heat (the sugar will continue to cook in the pan even though the heat is off). Once the temperature reaches 350°F (this will take only a few minutes), whisk in the butter, ½ tablespoon (1 piece) at a time, waiting until each addition is completely incorporated before adding the next. Stir in the vanilla and the salt, and pour the caramel into a 10-inch cast iron skillet.

Cover the caramel with the sliced potatoes, starting in the center and overlapping in a spiraling outward circle as you go. Top with the puff pastry circle. Beat the egg and the milk together and brush over the pastry, and then sprinkle with the remaining 1 tablespoon of sugar. Bake until the edges are deep amber and the pastry is puffed and golden, 40 to 45 minutes. Remove from the oven and cool for 10 minutes before inverting onto a large plate (make sure the diameter of the plate is larger than 10 inches!). Slice into wedges and serve with or without ice cream.

SERVES 6

→TIP To make life easier, I use store-bought puff pastry. Try to source an all-butter kind, like Dufour®, which gives the tart a rich flavor and tender texture.

Coconut Cream Pie

❦❦❦❦❦❦❦❦❦❦❦❦❦❦❦❦❦❦❦

This is a good ol' southern dessert that I remember digging into as a kid at both diner counters and kitchen tables. You can leave out the coconut extract if you don't have any around, but your pie won't have that deep coconut intensity that I love so much.

Though she passed on long before I was born, my mom's mom felt quite strongly that butter and shortening should have equal representation in pie dough. My grandmother was apparently very passionate in this belief, one shared by her sister, The GAP, who passed the pie passion on to me. So what do I do? I go ahead and use all butter! What kind of rebel would I be if I followed everyone else's advice?

My advice to you should be followed, though: For the flakiest piecrust, make sure your ingredients are cold—meaning cold butter, ice water, and even flour that has been refrigerated for an hour prior to making the dough. And don't overmix the dough—if you do, it's sure to shrink.

❦❦❦❦❦❦❦❦❦❦❦❦❦❦❦❦❦❦❦

Coconut Cream Pie

FOR THE CRUST

1½ cups all-purpose flour plus extra for rolling

2 tablespoons sugar

½ teaspoon salt

1½ sticks (12 tablespoons) unsalted butter, cut into small cubes

5–7 tablespoons ice water

FOR THE FILLING

1 cup sweetened coconut flakes

2 cups whole milk

5 large egg yolks

½ cup sugar

¼ cup cornstarch

1 teaspoon vanilla extract

1 teaspoon coconut extract

2 tablespoons unsalted butter

1 cup heavy cream

FOR THE TOPPING

2 cups heavy cream

¼ cup confectioners' sugar

½ teaspoon vanilla extract

TO MAKE THE CRUST

Place the flour, sugar, and salt in the bowl of a food processor and pulse to combine. Add the butter and pulse until the smallest pieces are about the size of corn kernels, 10 to 12 pulses. Add 5 tablespoons of water and pulse until the dough is no longer dry (when squeezed in your hand, it should form a ball and hold its shape), 4 to 6 times (if the dough is still dry, add another tablespoon or two of ice water). Turn the dough out onto your work surface and use your hands to form it into a disk. Wrap the dough in plastic wrap and chill for at least 1 hour or up to 3 days (or freeze for up to 1 month; defrost in the refrigerator overnight before using).

Remove the dough from the refrigerator (if it has been chilled for more than a few hours you may need to let it sit out at room temperature for 5 minutes to soften before rolling). Generously flour your work surface and roll the dough into a 12-inch circle that is about ⅛ inch thick. Fold the dough into quarters and transfer to a 9½-inch pie plate. Unfold the dough and fit it into the edges of the pie plate, then trim off all but ¼ inch of the overhang. Using your thumb and index finger, pinch the pie dough together to form a granny crimp, working your way around the edges (the edge of the dough should slightly hang over the rim of the pie plate). Chill for at least 1 hour or up to 1 day before baking.

Heat the oven to 350°F. When ready to bake, use a fork to prick the bottom and sides of the crust, refrigerate for 15 minutes, and then line with a large piece of aluminum foil. Pour dry beans, rice, or pie weights into the pie shell and bake directly on the rack until light golden brown around the edges, about 25 minutes. Remove the pie plate from the oven and carefully remove the foil and pie weights from the crust. Place the pie plate back in the oven and bake until the bottom of the crust is golden and dry, an additional 10 to 12 minutes. Set aside to cool.

TO MAKE THE FILLING

Reduce the oven temperature to 325°F. Place the coconut flakes on a rimmed baking sheet and bake in the oven until fragrant and brown, about 15 minutes, stirring occasionally. Transfer to a small bowl. Bring the milk and ½ cup of the coconut flakes to a boil in a medium saucepan over medium-high heat. Turn off the heat, cover, and steep for 5 minutes. Meanwhile, whisk the yolks, sugar, and cornstarch together in a large bowl. While whisking constantly, strain a little of the hot milk into the eggs (discard the coconut); once the bottom of the bowl is warm, strain the rest of the milk into the bowl and then transfer the egg-milk mixture back into the saucepan. While stirring constantly, cook the mixture over low heat until it becomes thick, 1 to 2 minutes. Continue to cook until a few bubbles pop on the surface, 1 to 2 minutes longer. Remove from the heat and whisk in the extracts and butter. Pour into a clean large bowl, press a piece of plastic wrap directly onto the top of the coconut cream, and refrigerate for 1 hour.

After the coconut cream has chilled, make the whipped cream. Place 1 cup of heavy cream in the bowl of a stand mixer (or in a large bowl if using a hand mixer) and whip on high speed until the cream forms stiff peaks, about 2 minutes. Remove the coconut cream from the refrigerator and whisk in a quarter of the whipped cream until smooth. Using a rubber spatula, fold in half of the remaining whipped cream, and then repeat with the rest of whipped cream. Gently scrape the filling into the pie shell and smooth out the top. Press a piece of plastic wrap directly onto the filling and refrigerate.

TO MAKE THE TOPPING

Whip the 2 cups of heavy cream with the confectioners' sugar and vanilla until it forms medium-stiff peaks, about 1½ minutes. Spread over the top of the filling and sprinkle with the reserved toasted coconut. Coconut cream pie tastes best served the same day that it's made, but it will keep for up to 2 days in the refrigerator.

MAKES ONE 9½-INCH PIE

VARIATION

BANANA CREAM PIE

Make the pie crust as instructed on p. 44 and the banana pudding as instructed on p. 94. Peel and slice 2 medium bananas into ¼-inch-thick coins and toss them with 1 tablespoon of lemon juice. Lay them flat in the cooled pie crust and up its sides. Add enough pudding to generously fill the pie shell and top with whipped cream topping (follow the instructions above).

Nana's Banana Bread

⋖⋗⋖⋗⋖⋗⋖⋗⋖⋗⋖⋗⋖⋗⋖⋗⋖⋗⋖⋗⋖⋗⋖⋗⋖⋗⋖⋗⋖⋗

Banana bread was the only dessert that Nana, Aunt Boo's mother, would make. Nana, who lived in Bogalusa, was a tough woman, who without a doubt passed the fly swatter method of discipline down to Aunt Boo. Nana didn't tolerate any kidding around—she was a woman of resolve. She knew her banana bread was good, and she knew she made it well, so she stuck to it.

Nana was so eager to share her banana bread that she gave up her recipe to just about anyone who asked for it, and I simply don't trust it—I'm sure that the recipe I have from Aunt Boo was intentionally handed down by Nana a few ingredients shy of perfection. I can just picture Nana smirking in the great beyond as we all scramble to replicate her moist and just sweet enough banana bread.

Well, her recipe is the one that I based mine off of—I've tweaked it here and there to match my memories of what hers tasted like: redolent with banana, super moist and tender, and without any nuts to get in the way. While I haven't adopted her fly swatter principle, I happily keep her banana bread tradition alive. Here's the complete recipe!

⋖⋗⋖⋗⋖⋗⋖⋗⋖⋗⋖⋗⋖⋗⋖⋗⋖⋗⋖⋗⋖⋗⋖⋗⋖⋗⋖⋗⋖⋗

1	stick plus 2 tablespoons unsalted butter, at room temperature
1¾	cups plus 2 tablespoons all-purpose flour
½	teaspoon ground cinnamon
1	teaspoon baking soda
½	teaspoon salt
3	very ripe bananas
1	teaspoon lemon juice
½	cup sugar
½	cup packed light brown sugar
½	teaspoon vanilla extract
2	large eggs
¼	cup buttermilk

Heat the oven to 350°F. Grease the bottom and sides of a 9x3-inch loaf pan with the 2 tablespoons of butter. Add the 2 tablespoons of flour and shake the pan to evenly coat the bottom and sides; tap out any excess and set the pan aside.

Sift together the remaining 1¾ cups of flour, the cinnamon, baking soda, and salt in a large bowl and set aside. Peel the bananas and place them in a small bowl. Add the lemon juice and mash them together with the back of a spoon or a potato masher (you want a little texture—like semi-lumpy mashed potatoes). Set aside.

In the bowl of a stand mixer (or in a large bowl if using a hand mixer), beat the remaining 1 stick of butter, the sugars, and the vanilla extract on low speed until combined. Increase the speed to medium and beat until fluffy, 1½ to 2 minutes. Add the eggs, one at a time, beating thoroughly between each addition and scraping down the bottom and sides of the bowl as necessary. Reduce the speed to low. Add a third of the dry ingredients, mixing until just incorporated, and then pour in half of the buttermilk and mix. Repeat, ending with the remaining third of the flour mixture. When the dry ingredients are nearly incorporated, scrape in the banana mixture, beating until the batter is just mixed (no more than 10 seconds).

Transfer the batter to the prepared loaf pan, set it on a baking sheet, and bake until a cake tester inserted into the center comes out clean, 60 to 70 minutes. Remove from the oven and cool for 10 minutes before running a knife around the edges to release the cake from the sides. Invert the cake onto a wire cooling rack and cool for 50 minutes, and then wrap in plastic wrap (it will still be warm—this helps the cake stay moist) and store for up to 4 days.

MAKES ONE 9X3-INCH LOAF

Black & Blue Crumble

My family served crumbles, crisps, cobblers, and any other variation of baked fruit covered with a sweet topping you could dream up. Whether for parties or funerals, we used whatever fruit was in season at the time, from fall apples and pears to summer's juiciest peaches and the sweetest berries and cherries. Unlike many southerners, I pull back on the sugar in my baked fruit desserts. I'd rather it taste like fresh fruit than pie filling. In this version, I use blackberries and blueberries and oven-bake them until they barely burst open. Topped with some vanilla ice cream, it's a heartbeat shy of heaven.

Black & Blue Crumble

½ cup sliced almonds

¼ cup quick oats

4 tablespoons unsalted butter, at room temperature

¼–½ cup sugar

2 tablespoons light brown sugar

¼ teaspoon vanilla extract

½ cup all-purpose flour

¼ teaspoon ground cinnamon

⅛ teaspoon salt

1 pound (4 cups) blackberries

1 pound (4 cups) blueberries

Zest of ½ lemon plus 2 tablespoons lemon juice

Sugar (anywhere from 2 tablespoons to a heaping ¼ cup)

3 tablespoons cornstarch or tapioca flour

Ice cream or whipped cream for serving

Heat the oven to 325°F. Spread out the almonds in an even layer on a rimmed baking sheet and toast for 8 minutes. Add the oats and continue to toast until the almonds just start to color, 4 to 6 minutes longer. Remove, transfer to a medium bowl, and set aside. Increase the oven temperature to 350°F.

Using a whisk or a wooden spoon, beat the butter, ¼ cup of the sugar, and the light brown sugar together in a medium bowl until relatively smooth. Stir in the vanilla, and then, using a fork, stir in the flour, cinnamon, and salt. Scoop and stir the mixture until it is crumbly with large nuggets (squeeze some of the topping together in your hand, release, and break apart for extra-large nuggets). Freeze for 10 minutes, stir in the almonds and oats, cover with plastic wrap, and refrigerate until the filling is ready (the topping can be made up to 1 week in advance or frozen for up to 3 months; defrost the topping at room temperature for 20 minutes before using).

Place the berries, lemon zest, and lemon juice in a large bowl. Taste a berry and add enough sugar to lightly sweeten (2 tablespoons for sweet berries, up to a generous ¼ cup for tart berries). Add the cornstarch or tapioca flour, toss, and transfer the filling to an 8-inch-square baking dish. Evenly cover with the crisp topping, place on a rimmed baking sheet, and bake until the berry juices are bubbling but the berries still hold their shape, about 1 hour. Remove from the oven and serve slightly warm or completely cool, topped with ice cream or whipped cream.

SERVES 8

VARIATION

APPLE-PEAR CRUMBLE

Peal and core 1 pound of apples (preferably Braeburns) and 1 pound of ripe pears (preferably Bartletts or d'Anjous). Cut them into ¾-inch cubes and toss with 2 tablespoons of honey. Proceed with the recipe above, substituting the apple-pear mixture for the berries.

PEACH CRUMBLE

Score an X in the bottom of 2 pounds of ripe peaches and blanch them in boiling water until their skins loosen, 30 seconds to 1 minute. Peel, pit, and cut into ¾-inch cubes, toss with 2 tablespoons of honey, and proceed with the recipe above, substituting the peaches for the berries.

Lemon Icebox Pie

Clancy's is a super neighborhood-type spot on Annunciation Street frequented by lots of locals, myself included. It's not a Galatoire's-like institution, but it has a loyal following nonetheless. It's intimate, with low ceilings, and has an amazing jovial vibe that always makes me feel right at home. In the ten years since I've lived in New Orleans, I can't remember a trip back to the city that didn't include at least one dinner at Clancy's—and at that dinner, I always order the same things: the fried eggplant, the sweetbreads, and the lemon icebox pie. My wife and I always share dessert, and this is one of the few that we actually fight over. While we'll happily listen to the waiter's dessert specials, our mind is made up the second we walk through the door: lemon icebox. As for making this at home, it just doesn't get any easier. It's simple and quick, plus it keeps in the freezer for over a week; it's a great dessert to make ahead for a dinner party. For a creamy key lime pie–like texture, let it sit out for 10 or 15 minutes before slicing.

Lemon Icebox Pie

FOR THE CRUST

14	whole graham crackers
¼	cup sugar
¼	teaspoon salt
6	tablespoons unsalted butter, melted and still warm

FOR THE FILLING

2	(14-ounce) cans condensed milk
1¼	cups strained lemon juice (from the 2 zested lemons below plus an additional 4–6)
	Zest of 2 lemons
8	large egg yolks

FOR THE CHANTILLY CREAM

2	cups heavy cream
½	teaspoon vanilla extract
¼	cup confectioners' sugar

TO MAKE THE CRUST

Heat the oven to 325°F. Break the graham crackers into small pieces and place in the bowl of a food processor along with the sugar and salt. Pulse 8 times, until the cracker crumbs are semi-fine (they shouldn't be powdery but not in large shards either) and the crackers and sugar are combined. Pour in the butter and pulse until the butter is blended in and the mixture isn't crumbly and holds its shape when you squeeze it, about twelve 1-second pulses. Transfer the crust to a 9-inch spring-form pan and push and press the crumb mixture into the bottom and two-thirds of the way up the sides of the pan. Use the bottom of a measuring cup to press the crust into place. Set aside.

TO MAKE THE FILLING

Whisk the condensed milk with the lemon juice and set aside. Whisk the zest with the egg yolks in a medium bowl until pale, 30 to 60 seconds, and then whisk in the lemon juice-condensed milk mixture.

Place the springform pan on a rimmed baking sheet, pour the mixture into the crust, and carefully transfer the baking sheet to the oven. Bake until the center jiggles slightly, like a soft-setting custard, about 25 minutes. Remove from the oven and cool for 1 hour on a cooling rack. Loosely cover the pan with plastic wrap (be careful not to let the plastic wrap touch the top of the pie) and freeze for at least 6 hours or overnight.

TO MAKE THE CHANTILLY CREAM

Pour the heavy cream into the bowl of a stand mixer (or in a large bowl if using a hand mixer). Add the vanilla and sift in the confectioners' sugar. Whip on low speed to combine and then increase the speed to medium-high and whip until medium-stiff peaks form, about 1½ minutes.

Before serving, wrap a wet, warm kitchen towel around the edges of the spring-form pan to release the pie from the pan's sides. Unclasp the pan and remove the pie. Fill a pitcher with hot water, dunk your knife in, wipe off the blade, and slice. Top with a dollop of chantilly cream and serve immediately, or keep in the freezer for up to 1 week.

MAKES ONE 9-INCH PIE

Cakes

IN ALL
SHAPES

Layers, Loaves & All Cakes in Between

To put it plainly, I bake cakes to fill the void in the pit of my stomach that makes me ache for home. I grew up with these cakes, the multilayered Doberge, scarlet wedges of red velvet, and homey slices of strawberry shortcake. Slicing a healthy slab with the side of a fork—whether at the dinner table, as part of a holiday celebration, or just any day at all—and tasting tender crumb against chocolate or slick icing or ripe fruit bring me straight back to my youth. Add a frosty glass of milk and you've got the best remedy for homesickness ever invented.

Red Velvet Cake

Red velvet is what I like to call a "feature" cake. It's the dessert that everyone oohs and aahs over—it's tall, dark, and handsome, with deep crimson cake layers and a thick coating of cream cheese frosting above, around, and between. It's about as southern as a cake can be, and I don't know anyone from Georgia to Texas who doesn't have a granny who makes "the best" one.

Now brace yourselves—mine veers from tradition. While customarily just a couple of tablespoons of cocoa get added to the batter, I throw in a whole one-half cup, giving the cake this delicious devil's food-like flavor and a deep crimson color. It's really rich and decadent, and even big eaters will be all set with a small slice. Unlike many cakes that dry out over time, this one just continues to get better, moister, and more delicious the longer it sits in the fridge. So don't be too shy to bake a cake for four (or two) devotees—you'll be enjoying it for days to come.

Red Velvet Cake

FOR THE CAKE

2	sticks plus 2 tablespoons unsalted butter, at room temperature
3	cups plus ¼ cup all-purpose flour
½	cup Dutch-processed cocoa powder
1½	teaspoons baking powder
1½	teaspoons baking soda
½	teaspoon salt
1	(1-pound) box light brown sugar (about 2¼ cups)
3	tablespoons red food coloring
2½	teaspoons vanilla extract
3	large eggs
1¾	cups buttermilk

FOR THE FROSTING

1¼	pounds cream cheese, at room temperature
2½	sticks unsalted butter, at room temperature
2	teaspoons vanilla extract
1	(2-pound) bag confectioners' sugar (about 7¼ cups)

TO MAKE THE CAKE

Heat the oven to 350°F. Grease two 9-inch cake pans with 1 tablespoon of butter each. Add 2 tablespoons of the flour to each pan and shake the pans to coat the bottom and sides. Tap out the excess flour and set the pans aside.

Sift the remaining 2¼ cups of flour with the cocoa, baking powder, baking soda, and salt, and set aside.

In the bowl of a stand mixer (or in a large bowl if using a hand mixer) cream the remaining butter with the brown sugar, food coloring, and vanilla on low to combine. Increase the mixer speed to medium-high and beat until aerated and pale, about 2 minutes. Reduce the speed to medium and add the eggs, one at a time, beating thoroughly between each addition and using a rubber spatula to scrape the sides and bottom of the bowl as necessary. Reduce the speed to low and add one-third of the dry ingredients followed by half of the buttermilk. Repeat, finishing with the final third of the dry mix. Scrape down the bottom and sides of the bowl and divide the batter between the two prepared cake pans, spreading it out as evenly as possible.

Bake until a cake tester inserted into the center comes out clean and the center of the cake resists slight pressure, about 40 minutes. Cool on a wire rack for 15 minutes, and then run a paring knife around the edges of each pan to release the cake from the sides; invert the cakes onto the cooling rack. Cool for 1 hour, and then wrap each cake in plastic wrap for at least a few hours.

TO MAKE THE FROSTING

Beat the cream cheese, butter, and vanilla together in the bowl of a stand mixer (or in a large bowl if using a hand mixer) on low speed to combine. Increase the speed to medium-high and beat until aerated and light, about 2 minutes. Stop the mixer and add a few cups of the confectioners' sugar, incorporating it into the cream cheese mixture on low speed until combined. Repeat with the remaining sugar, adding it to the mixer in two additions. Once all of the sugar is added, increase the speed to medium-high and beat until fluffy, about 1 minute.

TO ASSEMBLE THE CAKE

Unwrap the cake layers. Slice off the rounded top ⅛ inch of each cake and place the trimmed-away portion in the bowl of a food processor. Slice each cake in half horizontally (you'll end up with 4 layers), working over a baking sheet to catch any crumb (see p. 63 for tips on cutting even layers). Add the crumbs to the food processor and pulse until fine.

Place one cake layer on a cake round or large plate (make sure that the diameter of the plate is at least 1 inch larger than the cake). Use an offset spatula to evenly spread a heaping ¾ cup of frosting on the first cake layer. Repeat with the remaining three cake layers, ending with a bottom half of a cake on top, browned-side up (so you don't get cake crumbs in the frosting). Spread the remaining frosting over the top and sides of the cake (the sides don't have to look perfect—you're going to cover them with cake crumbs anyway). Gently press a handful of the reserved crumbs into the side of the cake until all of the sides are evenly coated. Refrigerate for at least 2 hours before serving.

MAKES ONE 9-INCH CAKE

➔MAKE AHEAD You can make the cake layers up to 3 days in advance. The filled and frosted cake keeps for up to 3 days in the refrigerator. Let it stand at room temperature for at least 20 minutes before slicing.

VARIATION

RED VELVET CUPCAKES

Follow the recipe on the facing page, making a half-batch of the batter (unless you have two 12-cup muffin tins, in which case you can make a full-size batch) and decreasing the baking powder to 1 teaspoon. Bake until the cupcakes are domes and resist slight pressure, 12 to 15 minutes. Cool completely before frosting with a half batch of the cream cheese frosting.

Lemon Doberge Cake

(Say it: DOUGH-bash)

Doberge cake is *the* birthday cake of New Orleans (though sometimes my sister, Tracy, and I did opt for a chocolate chip cookie cake; see p. 65). Gambino's, Haydel's, and probably every bakery in the city offers their take on the filled and stacked layer cake, with the most popular option being the half-and-half, a Doberge with a lemon-chocolate split personality—literally, a lemon-filled and-iced cake on one side, and a chocolate-filled and-iced cake on the other. This is my take on this truly New Orleans recipe.

Lemon Doberge Cake

FOR THE CAKE

2	sticks unsalted butter plus 2 tablespoons, melted, plus 2 tablespoons, at room temperature
1¾	cups plus 2 tablespoons all-purpose flour
1½	teaspoons baking powder
¾	teaspoon salt
1	teaspoon vanilla extract
6	large eggs
1¾	cups sugar
¾	cup whole milk
2	cups prepared lemon curd or ½ recipe Lemon Curd (p. 128)

FOR THE ICING

1	stick unsalted butter, at room temperature
4	cups confectioners' sugar
¼	cup lemon juice
2	drops yellow food coloring

Heat the oven to 350°F. Grease a 9-inch springform pan with the 2 tablespoons of room-temperature butter. Add the 2 tablespoons of flour and shake the pan to coat the bottom and sides, discarding the excess. Wrap the outside of the bottom of the pan in aluminum foil.

Sift the remaining 1¾ cups of flour, the baking powder, and salt together and set aside. Stir the vanilla into the melted butter and set aside.

Fill a medium saucepan with water to a depth of 1 inch, bring to a simmer over high heat, and then reduce the heat to low. Whisk the eggs and sugar together in a large heatproof bowl and place it over the hot water. Constantly whisk the mixture until it is warm to the touch, about 3 minutes. Pour it into the bowl of a stand mixer (or leave it in the large bowl if using a hand mixer) and whip on high speed until cool and tripled in volume, about 3 minutes.

Reduce the mixer speed to medium low, slowly drizzle in the melted butter, and then remove the bowl from the mixer. Use a whisk to gently fold in a third of the dry ingredients followed by half of the milk. Repeat, ending with a third of the flour mixture. Use a rubber spatula to transfer the batter to the prepared cake pan.

Bake until a cake tester inserted into the center comes out clean and the center resists slight pressure, about 1 hour. Remove from the oven, set aside for 5 minutes, and then invert onto a cooling rack. Unclasp the pan sides, carefully remove them, and then allow the cake to cool completely.

Remove the metal springform pan bottom from the cake and divide it into 4 layers (see the tip on the facing page). Wash and dry the springform pan, reassemble, and coat the bottom and sides with nonstick cooking spray. Place two 20-inch-long pieces of plastic wrap in the pan so the entire bottom and sides are covered, allowing the ends of the plastic wrap to hang over the sides of the pan. Place 1 cake layer in the springform pan and top with one-third of the lemon curd. Use the back of a spoon or an offset icing spatula to spread the curd evenly over the cake layer, leaving a ½-inch border of bare cake around the edge. Repeat with the remaining cake layers and lemon curd. Cover the top of the cake with the plastic wrap overhang (or an extra piece of plastic wrap if there isn't enough overhang to completely cover the cake) and refrigerate for at least 4 hours or overnight.

After the cake has chilled, make the icing. In the bowl of a stand mixer (or in a large bowl if using a hand mixer), mix the butter and sugar together on low speed until combined. Add the lemon juice and food coloring and mix on low speed until moistened, then increase the speed to medium and beat until creamy, about 2 minutes. Reduce the speed to low, add 1 tablespoon of warm water, and beat until fully incorporated, about 1 minute longer.

→TIP I can't say I have any tricks up my sleeve when it comes to dividing a cake into layers. Here's the method I learned eons ago. It has served me well.

After turning the cake out of the pan, use a serrated bread knife to make a small horizontal slit in the cake halfway up its side. Using very light pressure, cut into the cake one-quarter of the way. Keep your knife in that spot while giving the cake a quarter turn. Continue cutting and turning until your knife divides the cake into two layers. Repeat with each layer so you end up with four layers.

For an even easier experience, wrap your original uncut cake layer tightly in plastic wrap and refrigerate overnight before cutting the layers. This gives the butter a chance to tighten up, yielding a firmer cake that isn't so crumbly and delicate.

Place four 6-inch-wide strips of parchment paper around the edges of a flat plate or cake plate (some of the parchment paper should hang off the edge of the plate so you can pull the paper out from under the cake once it is frosted; the parchment keeps the plate clean while you ice the cake). Unfold the plastic from the top of the cake and invert the cake onto the parchment-lined plate. Unhinge the sides of the pan and remove completely. Peel off the plastic wrap. Use an offset spatula to ice the top and sides of the cake. Refrigerate for at least 1 hour and remove the parchment paper before serving. Doberge cake can be served cold, or you can let it sit at room temperature for up to 1 hour before serving.

MAKES ONE 9-INCH CAKE

→MAKE AHEAD The baked cake can be stored for up to 1 day (store whole, not divided into layers). Wrap in plastic and keep at room temperature. The filled and frosted cake keeps for up to 3 days in the refrigerator.

VARIATION

CHOCOLATE DOBERGE CAKE

Follow the recipe for the Lemon Doberge Cake, substituting 2 cups of prepared chocolate pudding (p. 95) for the lemon curd. To make a chocolate ganache icing, bring 1½ cups of heavy cream to a boil in a medium saucepan. Pour the hot cream over 12 ounces of finely chopped semisweet chocolate and set the bowl aside for 2 minutes. Begin whisking the mixture from the center until smooth, and then begin bringing the liquid from the sides of the bowl toward the center, whisking until the ganache has a nice sheen and is completely smooth. Whisk in 2 tablespoons of softened unsalted butter and press a piece of plastic wrap directly onto the surface of the ganache. Set aside for at least 6 hours (or overnight) before giving the ganache a gentle swirl and frosting the top and sides of the cake with an offset spatula. After frosting, refrigerate the cake for at least 1 hour or up to 3 days before slicing and serving. As with the lemon Doberge, the cake can be served cold or at room temperature.

DOBERGE CAKE:
THE BIRTHDAY CAKE OF NEW ORLEANS

New Orleanians can thank Beulah Ledner, who began baking out of her house during the Great Depression as a way to pay the bills, for the Doberge cake. The Doberge is a riff on the Austrian Dobos Torte, a cake made of nine génoise cake layers bound together by buttercream and covered with a hard caramel glaze. Ms. Ledner replaced the buttercream filling with a custard one, instead using buttercream to frost the cake and finishing it off with a thin layer of fondant all around.

According to legend, Ms. Ledner sold her recipe and bakery to the Gambino family in the 1940s. The Gambinos still have a corner on the Doberge market (you can even order the cake online at www.gambinos.com). Ms. Ledner's book, *Let's Bake with Beulah Ledner*, was published in 1987 by Maxine Wolchansky (Southern Graphics) and includes her recipe for the now legendary cake.

Chocolate Chip Cookie Cake

When I didn't get a Doberge cake (see p. 60) for my birthday, I got a chocolate chip cookie cake. It was the best—a giant chocolate chip sheet cake, with my name piped on it in chocolate frosting. My mom would order the cake from some shop long gone now. She'd arrive home from the store with the cake securely enclosed in a white pizza-like box. We'd cut the cake into small squares and serve pieces to all my friends. Soft and tender, this birthday cake is still a sweet I look forward to baking for (and eating with!) my boys.

I based mine on my recipe for chocolate chip cookies baked in a cake pan rather than in individual knobs. The almond extract adds a nice sweetness that I like, but if you don't have any, you can leave it out. This dough makes great chocolate chip cookies, too.

Chocolate Chip Cookie Cake

2 cups (12 ounces) semisweet chocolate chips or chunks (58%–62% cacao), roughly chopped

½ cup heavy cream

1 stick plus 1½ tablespoons unsalted butter, at room temperature

1 cup all-purpose flour

1½ teaspoons baking powder

¼ teaspoon salt

1 cup light brown sugar

1 teaspoon vanilla extract

½ teaspoon almond extract

1 large egg

To make the ganache, place ¾ cup of the chocolate in a small bowl. Bring the cream to a boil over medium-high heat and pour it over the chocolate. Cover with plastic wrap and set aside for 3 minutes, then whisk it from the center of the bowl out to the edges until smooth (don't vigorously whisk the chocolate mixture—you don't want to whip in air bubbles). Re-cover with plastic wrap and set aside at room temperature for at least 6 hours or overnight.

To make the cookie cake, heat the oven to 350°F. Place a 10-inch cake pan on top of a piece of parchment paper and trace a circle. Cut the circle out and set aside. Grease the 10-inch cake pan with the 1½ tablespoons of softened butter, and then press the parchment circle into the pan. Grease the top of the parchment with a little more butter and set the pan aside.

Whisk the flour, baking powder, and salt together in a medium bowl and set aside. Using a stand mixer or a hand mixer, cream the stick of butter, light brown sugar, and vanilla and almond extracts on medium speed until well combined, about 1 minute. Increase the mixer speed to high and beat for 15 seconds. Stop the mixer, scrape down the sides of the bowl, and add the egg. Blend on medium speed for 30 seconds. Add the dry ingredients and combine on low speed until just a few dry streaks remain. Add the remaining chopped chocolate and mix for a few seconds until combined.

Scrape the batter into the prepared cake pan. Dip a rubber spatula in cold water, shake off the excess, and use it to press the batter into a smooth and even layer in the pan. Bake until lightly golden and puffy around the edges (the center should still feel quite soft), 18 to 22 minutes. Cool for 10 minutes and then run a paring knife around the edge of the pan to release the cake. Cool for at least 4 hours before turning the cake out of the pan and onto a large plate (or cutting board). Peel off the parchment, then invert back onto a cake plate or stand.

Use a rubber spatula to fill a pastry bag fitted with an 8-mm tip (or a resealable plastic bag with one corner snipped off) with the ganache. Pipe a decorative border around the edge of the cake and streak the remaining ganache across the entire cake, or write the name of the recipient in the center.

MAKES ONE 10-INCH CAKE

→MAKE AHEAD Ganache needs to set up for a while to thicken before you can pipe with it. I often make it the night before I plan on using it (cover it flush with plastic wrap and leave it at room temperature). The cake keeps covered (a large, inverted metal mixing bowl works well as a lid), and at room temperature, for up to 1 day.

Buttermilk Drops

Every Sunday before church, and sometimes even before the sun came up, my grandfather picked me up to get pastries at McKenzie's bakery. I'd swagger up to the display case and stare down the sweets like a cowboy in the Wild West. On the mornings when I didn't go for éclairs I'd go for buttermilk drops, baseball-size cake donuts so darn good I'd down four of them without batting an eye. Swathed in a light coating of donut glaze that collected in the nooks and crannies like a good old-fashioned cruller, at first bite they'd yield a good dose of sweet icing, and then you'd taste the tingly acidity of the interior. Oh boy, they were heaven in a handful. Though McKenzie's is long gone, I've tried to replicate my memory of their buttermilk drops here. I make them a little smaller, so you get the perfect ratio of glaze to donut in every bite.

FOR THE DONUTS

6	cups peanut or vegetable oil
1	cup all-purpose flour
1	tablespoon sugar
1	teaspoon baking powder
¼	teaspoon baking soda
½	teaspoon ground ginger
½	teaspoon freshly grated nutmeg
¼	teaspoon salt
½	cup buttermilk
1	large egg
1	large egg yolk
1	teaspoon lemon juice
3	tablespoons unsalted butter, melted

FOR THE GLAZE

2	cups confectioners' sugar
3–4	tablespoons buttermilk
½	teaspoon vanilla extract

→TIP Dip the spoon into the hot oil before scooping the donut batter. The oil-greased spoon will allow the batter to effortlessly roll right off and into the hot oil.

Pour enough of the oil into a large pot to fill it to a 2½- to 3-inch depth and bring it to a temperature between 350°F and 360°F over medium heat (see "How to Fry," p. 29). Line a plate with paper towels and set aside.

While the oil heats up, make the glaze. Whisk the confectioners' sugar, vanilla, and 3 tablespoons of the buttermilk together in a medium bowl (if the batter looks too thick and pasty, add the remaining tablespoon of buttermilk). Set aside.

To make the donuts, whisk the flour, sugar, baking powder, baking soda, ginger, nutmeg, and salt together in a large bowl. Create a well in the center of the dry ingredients. Whisk the buttermilk, egg, egg yolk, and lemon juice together in a small bowl. Pour into the center of the dry ingredients. Begin whisking the mixture from the center of the well until smooth, and then gradually bring in the dry ingredients from around the sides of the bowl, whisking until well combined. Stir in the melted butter.

Once your oil is hot, scoop out a tablespoon of batter. Hold the spoon close to the oil and let the batter roll off the spoon and into the oil; repeat with the remaining batter (the donuts should be able to freely bob around in the oil; take care not to overcrowd the pot, otherwise the oil will cool and the donuts will take longer to fry, yielding a greasy donut). Using a slotted spoon, turn and baste the donuts occasionally, allowing them to become deep brown on all sides. (Fry the donuts in two batches if your pot becomes overcrowded.) If the temperature of the oil dips below 350°F, increase the heat to medium-high. Fry, turning often to ensure even browning, until the donuts are a deep, nutty brown color, 4 to 5 minutes. Use a slotted spoon or frying spider to transfer to the prepared plate.

Place a cooling rack over a sheet pan and set aide. Stir the glaze. While the donuts are still warm, dunk each one in the glaze, rolling it around with a spoon to make sure it gets an even coating. Transfer the glazed donuts to the cooling rack and set aside for 20 minutes before eating.

MAKES ABOUT 20 DONUTS

Ponchatoula Strawberry
& Brown Butter Shortcake

This strawberry shortcake was inspired by the shortcakes I ate as a kid at the Ponchatoula Strawberry Festival. Every February, usually around Mardi Gras time, I'd shake off my city stigmata and embrace my inner country bumpkin, from watching the parade and the crowning of the Strawberry King and Queen to climbing into a muddy corral to catch a greased pig! Of course the food was the biggest draw of all, with booths lined up shoulder-to-shoulder and people queuing for strawberry short-cake as if the vendor was giving away money rather than selling dessert. I'd start with some gumbo or a crisp, buttered breadcrumb–topped shrimp casserole and then move on to strawberry pudding, strawberry ice cream, and, of course, strawberry shortcake, made with a mound of sticky-sweet berries atop a tender southern biscuit, the whole shebang finished with freshly whipped cream.

Instead of biscuits, try this tender, spongy brown butter cake to act as the cushion to the berries. It's nice because the cake stays delicious for a couple of days, so you can bake it ahead of time if you're having company over (biscuits need to be served within an hour—preferably minutes—of baking). Many cooks strain their browned butter to remove the browned milk solids before using. I don't—I think those little dark bits are pure magic that lend amazingly complex and wonderful flavors to this dessert.

Ponchatoula Strawberry Shortcake

2　pounds (6 cups) strawberries, hulled and quartered if large

Zest of 1 orange

1¼　cups sugar

1½　sticks plus 1 tablespoon unsalted butter

1　cup plus 2 tablespoons all-purpose flour

4　large eggs

1　teaspoon baking powder

¼　teaspoon salt

½　cup buttermilk

Chantilly cream (p. 53) for serving

→TIP While I like serving the strawberries on top of brown butter shortcake, if you prefer a biscuit to cake, check out the recipe on p. 137.

Bring a large pot with 1 inch of water to a simmer over medium-high heat. Stir the strawberries, orange zest, and ¼ cup of the sugar in a large stainless steel mixing bowl, cover with plastic wrap, and place on top of the pot (the bottom of the bowl shouldn't touch the water). Reduce the heat to low and let the strawberries macerate over the simmering water for 20 minutes. Remove the bowl from the pot (leave the pot and water on the stove but turn off the heat) and refrigerate until chilled (the strawberry sauce can be made up to 1 day in advance).

Heat the oven to 350°F. Place a 10-inch cake pan on parchment; trace and cut out a circle. Grease the pan's bottom and sides with the tablespoon of butter, press the parchment into the pan, and flip the parchment over, buttered side up. Add 2 tablespoons of flour and tap to coat the bottom and sides; discard the excess.

Cut the remaining 1½ sticks of butter into small pieces and melt in a medium saucepan over medium-high heat. Simmer, whisking often to incorporate any solids that sink to the bottom, until the butter is a golden-amber color and smells nutty, 4 to 6 minutes. If it sputters or spatters, reduce the heat. Set the butter aside to cool.

Bring the pot with water back to a simmer over medium-high heat. Whisk the eggs and remaining sugar together in a large heatproof bowl and place over the pot of water (the bottom of the bowl should not touch the water). Reduce the heat to low and whisk the mixture until it has tripled in volume, 4 to 5 minutes.

Transfer the mixture to the bowl of a stand mixer (or into a large bowl if using a hand mixer) and whip on high speed until it is thick, and pale, 2 to 3 minutes. Meanwhile, sift the remaining 1 cup of flour, the baking powder, and salt together. Reduce the speed of the mixer to low and slowly drizzle in the warm butter (adding it too quickly will cause the batter to separate), using a rubber spatula to scrape the browned bits into the batter. Turn off the mixer. Using a whisk, gently fold in one-third of the dry ingredients, fold in half of the buttermilk, and then repeat, ending with the last third of the dry mixture, gently folding in until just combined.

Transfer the batter to the prepared cake pan, tilting the pan to make sure the batter spreads evenly. Bake until the cake sides pull away from the pan and the center resists light pressure, 22 to 26 minutes. Remove from the oven and let it rest for 10 minutes before running a paring knife around the edges of the pan to release the shortbread and inverting it onto a cooling rack to cool completely.

Transfer the cake to a plate and slice into wedges. Serve topped with strawberries, sauce, and a dollop of chantilly cream, or slice each wedge in half horizontally and sandwich the halves with strawberries and sauce, then top with cream.

SERVES 8

Gâteau de Sirop

(Say it: gat-TOE de sir-up)

In Louisiana, fall means it's cane syrup season. That's when sugarcane from the fields of Abbeville, Breaux Bridge, and New Iberia, among countless others, is harvested, stripped, and boiled down in open kettles into a thick sticky-sweet mass called cane syrup. Kind of like the love child of molasses and sorghum, cane syrup is the key ingredient to this cake. Served warm with plenty more syrup poured over the top (you Yankees can drizzle your hearts out—we Louisianans upturn and pour), it's layered comfort on a plate. Gâteau de Sirop screams holiday-time to me and mine, and I think it is hands-down the best darn gingerbread on earth. With loads of fresh, grated ginger to cut the maltiness of the cane syrup (see p. 165 for more on cane syrup) and a dash of Crystal® hot sauce for good measure, a hulking slice brings me straight to Vermilion Parish. Topped with a scoop of vanilla ice cream, it's hard to beat.

Gâteau de Sirop

1 piece fresh ginger, about 4 inches long, peeled and grated

1 tablespoon unsalted butter, at room temperature

2½ cups plus 2 tablespoons all-purpose flour

2 teaspoons baking soda

½ teaspoon ground cinnamon

¼ teaspoon salt

1½ cups Steen's cane syrup plus extra for serving (optional)

1 cup peanut oil or vegetable oil

1 cup light brown sugar

1 teaspoon hot sauce (preferably Crystal's)

2 large eggs

Place the ginger in a small saucepan. Pour 1 cup of water over the ginger and bring the mixture to a boil over medium-high heat. Turn off the heat and let the ginger steep for 5 minutes, and then strain the mixture through a fine-mesh sieve placed over a bowl. Press on the ginger to extract all the liquid, discard the ginger pulp, and set the ginger water aside.

Heat the oven to 350°F. Grease a 9-inch cake pan with the butter. Add the 2 tablespoons of flour to the pan and shake to coat the bottom and sides. Tap out the excess and set the pan aside. Whisk the remaining 2½ cups of flour, the baking soda, cinnamon, and salt together in a large bowl and set aside.

Pour 1 cup of the cane syrup, the oil, brown sugar, ginger water, and hot sauce into the bowl of a stand mixer (or into a large bowl if using a hand mixer) and whisk to combine. Whisk in the eggs one at a time and add the dry ingredients all at once. Using the paddle attachment, beat the mixture on low speed until the batter is smooth, 2 to 3 minutes. Scrape the sides and bottom of the bowl using a rubber spatula and then pour the batter into the prepared cake pan.

Bake until a cake tester inserted into the center of the cake comes out clean and the center resists slight pressure, about 1 hour. Place the cake on a cooling rack to cool for 15 minutes. Using a cake tester or a fork, poke lots of holes into the top of the cake going all the way through to just shy of the bottom of the cake. Pour the remaining ½ cup of cane syrup over the top of the cake and let it sit for at least 1 hour before slicing. Serve straight from the pan while still warm or at room temperature with extra cane syrup poured over the top. You can also unmold it for presentation, but be sure to pour more cane syrup over it before serving.

MAKES ONE 9-INCH CAKE

→MAKE AHEAD The cake keeps for up to 3 days if wrapped tightly in plastic. Keep it in the cake pan to prevent it from drying out; do not refrigerate.

Sweet Corn Cake
with Root Beer Syrup

Soft, rich, and absolutely wonderful, why not serve a spoonbread-style cake as a dessert instead of as a savory side? Baked in a cast iron skillet, this dessert is super homey. How does it differ from cornbread? It has sugar in it! In my world, cake is cake, and bread is bread—you can dress up cornbread with honey, molasses, sorghum, or cane syrup, but as long as the sweetener is on the outside it's a bread. With 1 cup of sugar in the batter, my version is definitely a cake. To give it a little more oomph, I add bourbon and then drizzle the finished cake with a reduced root beer syrup (often my hometown favorite, Abita®). Straight up Steen's Cane Syrup is awesome poured over the top, too. Serve with a scoop of vanilla ice cream and call it a day.

2	tablespoons unsalted butter, at room temperature
¾	cup plus 2 tablespoons all-purpose flour
2½	teaspoons baking powder
¼	teaspoon salt
½	cup fine yellow cornmeal
¼	cup bourbon (preferably Maker's Mark®)
1	cup corn oil
6	large egg yolks
3	large eggs
1	cup sugar
2¼	cups (20 ounces) root beer (preferably Abita)
	Vanilla ice cream for serving

Heat the oven to 350°F. Grease a 10-inch cast iron skillet with the butter. Add the 2 tablespoons of flour and shake and tap to evenly coat the bottom and sides of the skillet. Shake out the excess flour and set the skillet aside.

Sift the remaining ¾ cup of flour, the baking powder, and salt into a large bowl, and then whisk in the cornmeal and set aside. Whisk the bourbon and oil together and set aside. Place the egg yolks, eggs, and sugar in the bowl of a stand mixer (or in a large bowl if using a hand mixer) and whip on high speed until pale yellow and thick, about 3 minutes. Reduce the speed to low and add one-third of the dry ingredients followed by half of the bourbon-oil mixture. Repeat, finishing with the final third of the dry mix. Scrape down the bottom and sides of the bowl and pour the batter into the prepared cast iron skillet. Bake until the cake is golden brown and the center resists light pressure, 40 to 45 minutes.

Remove the cake from the oven and cool until the sides begin to pull away, about 5 minutes. Run a paring knife around the edges of the pan to release the cake from the sides, then flip it out onto a cooling rack. Cool completely.

While the cake cools, make the root beer syrup. Pour the root beer into a heavy-bottomed saucepan over medium-high heat. Bring it to a simmer, and then reduce the heat to low and continue to cook the root beer until it is reduced to ½ cup, 45 minutes to 1 hour. Turn off the heat and keep at room temperature until you serve the cake. Slice the cake into 12 pieces and top with the root beer syrup and a scoop of vanilla ice cream.

MAKES ONE 10-INCH CAKE

➤MAKE AHEAD The root beer syrup can be made up to a few days ahead. Store it in a small gravy boat or creamer covered in plastic wrap. Microwave for a few seconds if it doesn't pour easily. Different brands of root beer will yield varying syrup thicknesses—for example, A&W® makes a thinner syrup while Barq's® is on the heavier side. If you can't find Abita, try to go with Barq's.

TAG's PB Brownies

❖⟡❖⟡❖⟡❖⟡❖⟡❖⟡❖⟡❖⟡❖⟡❖⟡❖⟡❖⟡❖⟡❖⟡❖⟡❖

When we were kids, my sister, Tracy, and I would really cut loose in the kitchen. With a box of brownie mix, we could come up with the craziest concoctions, adding everything from M&Ms® to grape jelly to our brownie batter. Not all the batches came out good (there's a blueberry batch that I recall being particularly inedible), but once in a while we'd hit a winner, like these peanut butter brownies. While I haven't used a brownie mix in ages (I've since come up with my own recipe for super rich and chocolatey brownies), I still love adding peanut butter to these chocolatey chunks of bliss. That said, whenever I bake up a pan, I always think of Tracy. So it's to her that I dedicate this recipe. I don't think she'll mind that I borrowed her initials—TAG—to title it.

A word of caution: You should really have someone else present when you're eating these brownies. Otherwise, you could easily eat half a pan before you realize what you've done. Be sure to have some ice-cold milk ready to go in a tumbler (or freeze a beer mug for a super frosty glass of milk). You'll need it.

❖⟡❖⟡❖⟡❖⟡❖⟡❖⟡❖⟡❖⟡❖⟡❖⟡❖⟡❖⟡❖⟡❖⟡❖⟡❖

1	stick unsalted butter, cut into small pieces
9	ounces bittersweet chocolate (preferably 66%–72% cacao), finely chopped
2	whole eggs
1	cup firmly packed light brown sugar
2	teaspoons vanilla extract
¼	teaspoon salt
⅓	cup all-purpose flour
⅓	cup smooth peanut butter

Heat the oven to 300°F. Grease an 8-inch-square baking dish with nonstick cooking spray, line with parchment paper, and spray the paper to lightly coat it. Bring 2 inches of water to a simmer in a medium saucepan over medium-high heat. Place the butter and chocolate in a medium heatproof bowl, and then place the bowl over the simmering water (the bottom of the bowl shouldn't touch the water). Reduce the heat to low and melt the butter and chocolate together, stirring often. Remove from the heat and whisk in the eggs, sugar, vanilla, and salt until completely incorporated. Whisk in the flour and scrape the mixture into the prepared pan, using a rubber spatula to evenly spread the batter and smooth the top.

Place the peanut butter in a quart-size resealable plastic bag and snip off one corner, making a ½-inch hole. Squeeze the peanut butter down into the cut corner of the bag and twist the top of the bag closed. Pipe the peanut butter in four long, straight lines across the top of the batter. Using a skewer, toothpick, or tip of a knife, swirl the peanut butter into the batter, just enough so it looks marbled. Bake until the chocolate portions of the brownie surface have a smooth sheen and are dry, about 45 minutes (the peanut butter portions will still be tacky). Let cool completely before slicing into 2-inch squares.

MAKES SIXTEEN 2-INCH SQUARES

→MAKE AHEAD The brownies will keep in the refrigerator for up to a week. Eat them cold (they're nice and fudgy) or let them warm up to room temperature before enjoying.

Chocolate Cupped Cakes
with Coffee & Chicory

꧁꧂꧁꧂꧁꧂꧁꧂꧁꧂꧁꧂꧁꧂꧁꧂꧁꧂꧁꧂

I'd often sneak into my mom's car and ride stowaway-style in the back seat when she left home to "make groceries" at the A&P or Schwegmann's. No sooner had she turned off the ignition than I'd pop my head up and scare the bejesus out of her! In the market, we'd get coffee beans ground fresh from this giant red coffee grinder—I swear it was at least 3 feet tall. My mom gave the coffee man (usually the bagger at the checkout aisle) explicit instructions on the coarseness of the bean grind for her chicory-laced coffee. After he had bagged our beans, I'd stick my nose up the metal spout and inhale the heady aroma that always made me dizzy and happy.

In a typical New Orleans home, a pitcher of coffee can almost always be found in the fridge, whether left over from the morning or brewed specifically to make iced coffee later in the day. This coffee and chicory cupped cake is made with a stiff, eggless cake batter that gets topped with a cocoa crumble and then covered with coffee. Baked in actual coffee cups, the cake soufflés up and makes its own built-in lava sauce on the bottom. It's fantastic eaten within an hour or two of baking while the cake is still warm, soft, and molten.

꧁꧂꧁꧂꧁꧂꧁꧂꧁꧂꧁꧂꧁꧂꧁꧂꧁꧂꧁꧂

Chocolate Cupped Cakes

2 cups plus 2 tablespoons sugar

¼ cup light brown sugar

½ cup Dutch-processed cocoa powder

3 tablespoons unsalted butter, at room temperature

1¼ cups heavy cream

1 teaspoon vanilla extract

2½ cups all-purpose flour

1 tablespoon instant espresso powder

2 teaspoons baking powder

½ teaspoon salt

1 cup brewed New Orleans–style chicory coffee

Heat the oven to 350°F. Spray the insides of 6 large oven-safe coffee cups or six 6-ounce ramekins with nonstick cooking spray and place on a rimmed baking sheet.

To make the cocoa sprinkle, whisk ¼ cup of the sugar, the light brown sugar, and 2 tablespoons of the cocoa powder in a small bowl until most of the brown sugar lumps are broken up, and set aside.

Using a stand mixer (or in a large bowl if using a hand mixer), blend the butter and remaining sugar together on medium speed until the sugar looks like wet sand, about 2 minutes. Reduce the speed to low and add the cream and vanilla, mixing until well blended, using a rubber spatula to scrape the sides of the bowl as necessary.

Whisk the flour, the remaining cocoa powder, espresso powder, baking powder, and salt together in a large bowl and then add it to the butter mixture. Mix on low speed until a stiff dough comes together, then increase the speed to medium and beat for 15 seconds.

Divide the batter between the coffee cups, filling each one about half full, using the back of a spoon to press the batter into the cup. Top each with 2 tablespoons of the reserved cocoa sprinkle and then pour 2½ tablespoons of coffee over the cocoa. Bake until the cakes soufflé up and the top of each cake is crusty and dry on top with no visible wet spots, about 55 to 60 minutes. Cool for at least 20 minutes before serving.

SERVES 6

→MAKE AHEAD This cake is best eaten warm within a few hours of baking. If you have some left over the next day, you can heat it up in the microwave before serving to get its gooey quality back.

→TIP You'll have a little of the cocoa sprinkle left over after making the cakes. Use it to top a scoop of ice cream or stir it into iced coffee (with condensed milk if you really want to go all out). If you don't have oven-safe coffee cups, you can make this cake in a 9-inch-square baking dish and serve it casserole style, scooped into dessert bowls (it may need an extra 5 to 10 minutes in the oven).

New Orleans' Coffee and Chicory Tradition

The port of New Orleans has been a site of international trade since 1718, with the first coffee shipments coming from Cuba and the Caribbean soon after. By the 1840s, the port was the largest importer of coffee after New York City, and today 250,000 tons of green coffee beans come through the port every year. With six roasting facilities located within 20 miles of the port (including the world's largest coffee bulk-processing operation), New Orleans remains the country's premiere entry point for coffee.

New Orleans' chicory tradition goes back hundreds of years, too. Perhaps New Orleanians got the idea of adding roasted and ground chicory to coffee from the French, who used the root to stretch their coffee supplies during the Napoleonic blockades of ports in the early 19th century. During

the Civil War, when Union naval blockades cut off the port of New Orleans, Louisianans began adding chicory root to their coffee—the difference is that we Louisianans became enamored of the sweet, nutty, toasty quality that chicory lent to our café au lait, so in typical New Orleanian style, we clung to the tradition with fierce loyalty. In fact, even though I haven't lived in New Orleans for a decade, I still am always sure to have a fresh-opened red bag of Community® Coffee New Orleans Blend® in my cabinet.

While chicory doesn't contain any caffeine whatsoever, it does give off more soluble matter, creating a darker, stronger-tasting cup of coffee while using fewer actual coffee beans. Go figure that now New Orleans-style chicory coffee often costs more than 100% Arabica!

SOFTIES AND Spoon Sweets

Puddings & Cup Custards

Something about puddings and custards is so soothing to me. I'd bet my Harley® that banana or vanilla pudding was one of the first sweets I ever tasted as a baby, so perhaps my comfort comes from these deep-seated memories. Though pudding is definitely a southern thing, as creamy and smooth as Dr. John gliding over the ivories, it's also a big part of my Cuban heritage. So between my dad's Latin side and my mom's Louisianan one, I was destined to be a champion of these simple and seductive spoon sweets.

Cup Custard

⋄⋅⋅⋅⋄⋅⋅⋅⋄⋅⋅⋅⋄⋅⋅⋅⋄⋅⋅⋅⋄⋅⋅⋅⋄⋅⋅⋅⋄⋅⋅⋅⋄⋅⋅⋅⋄⋅⋅⋅⋄⋅⋅⋅⋄⋅⋅⋅⋄⋅⋅⋅⋄⋅⋅⋅⋄

In France it's known as crème caramel, in Cuba it's flan. In New Orleans, we call it cup custard, because, well, it's custard made in a cup. In my house, my dad, who was born in Cuba, was the flan go-to guy, and I've been surrounded by this silky spoon sweet for as long as I can remember. For the Guas family, the test of a great flan was that it didn't show any signs of craters in the moon—a sure-tell that the custard is overbaked.

No different from its continental cousins, New Orleans cup custard is stiff enough to stand straight after unmolding and soft enough to make you sigh with each bite. The built-in caramel sauce that spills over the custard after you remove the ramekin is a major bonus, too.

⋄⋅⋅⋅⋄⋅⋅⋅⋄⋅⋅⋅⋄⋅⋅⋅⋄⋅⋅⋅⋄⋅⋅⋅⋄⋅⋅⋅⋄⋅⋅⋅⋄⋅⋅⋅⋄⋅⋅⋅⋄⋅⋅⋅⋄⋅⋅⋅⋄⋅⋅⋅⋄⋅⋅⋅⋄⋅⋅⋅⋄

Cup Custard

1 cup sugar
5 large eggs
3 large egg yolks
2 teaspoons vanilla extract
⅛ teaspoon salt
2 cups whole milk
2 cups heavy cream

→TIP Slippery ramekins are a giant pet peeve of mine. I discovered this cool trick to make your tongs nonslip: just wrap a thick rubber band around the lower scalloped portion of each tong half. The rubber acts like tread to the slippery ceramic ramekin.

Heat the oven to 325°F. Place ½ cup of the sugar and 2 tablespoons of water in a small saucepan. Gently stir with a spoon to make sure all of the sugar is wet (it should have the consistency of wet sand), place a cover on slightly askew, and bring to a boil over medium-high heat. Keep the mixture covered until the syrup is clear and producing syrupy-looking medium-size bubbles, 3 to 4 minutes. Remove the cover and continue to cook until the color of the sugar is a deep amber and the temperature reads 350°F, about 8 minutes. Remove from the heat and divide the caramel between six 5- to 6-ounce ramekins, place them in a 9x11-inch baking dish, and set aside.

Whisk the eggs, egg yolks, vanilla, and salt together in a large bowl. Stir the milk, cream, and remaining ½ cup of sugar together in a medium saucepan and bring to a boil over medium-high heat. While whisking, slowly pour the hot milk mixture into the egg mixture, until the bottom of the bowl is warm, then vigorously whisk in the remaining hot milk mixture. Pour through a fine-mesh sieve into a large measuring cup and evenly divide the liquid between the ramekins.

Pour enough water into the baking dish to come halfway up the sides of the ramekins (be careful not to get water in the ramekins). Cover the baking dish with a sheet of aluminum foil and poke six holes in the top to allow steam to vent out. Carefully transfer the dish to the oven and bake for 25 minutes. Turn one corner of the foil up to release the steam, re-cover, and rotate the dish. Bake until the surface of the custard is dry and a dime-size center portion gives a slight jiggle when a ramekin is tapped, about 15 minutes longer. Use tongs to remove the custards from the baking dish (see the tip at left) and place them on a rack to cool for 30 minutes before covering with plastic wrap and refrigerating for at least 8 hours or up to 3 days.

To serve, run a paring knife around the edge of the custard and place a plate (or shallow dessert bowl) on top of the ramekin. Invert the ramekin onto the plate; the custard should slip right out. Pour the caramel sauce from the ramekin over the custard and serve. (To clean the ramekin: If, after you've unmolded the custard, you're left with a hard sugar ring in the bottom, simply fill the ramekin with a little hot water and let it sit a spell. The sugar will effortlessly dissolve.)

MAKES 6 CUSTARDS

Vanilla Bean Pudding

While granny-style desserts like puddings have made a comeback to the white tablecloth setting, let me assure you that vanilla pudding was never meant to be a restaurant dessert. It was always something made by a momma in a home kitchen. That said, I can't stop myself from adding vanilla beans, a luxury ingredient that I never saw or used until I started working in professional kitchens. I love the slightly seedy texture the beans add and the look of the little black seeds suspended within the custard. If vanilla beans are hard to find in your neck of the woods, by all means use vanilla extract instead, but please read the back of the box to make sure it's the real deal and not imitation.

Vanilla Bean Pudding

5   large egg yolks

½   cup granulated sugar

¼   cup cornstarch

2   cups whole milk

1   vanilla bean (preferably Tahitian), split in half down the middle, seeds scraped from the bean and reserved, or 2 teaspoons vanilla extract

2   tablespoons unsalted butter

Whisk the egg yolks, sugar, and cornstarch together in a medium bowl and set aside. Bring the milk, vanilla bean, and the scraped seeds to a boil in a medium saucepan (if using vanilla extract, add it with the butter after cooking the pudding). Remove from the heat and whisk a little at a time into the egg mixture (discard the vanilla bean). Once the bottom of the bowl is warm, slowly whisk in the remaining hot milk. Pour the mixture back into a clean medium saucepan (cleaning the saucepan prevents the pudding from scorching) and whisk over medium-low heat until it thickens, about 2 minutes. Cook while constantly whisking until the pudding is glossy and quite thick, 1½ to 2 minutes longer. Transfer the pudding to a clean bowl. Whisk in the butter (and vanilla extract if using instead of vanilla bean) and press a piece of plastic wrap onto the surface of the pudding to prevent a skin from forming. Refrigerate for 4 hours.

Before serving, whisk the pudding until it is soft and smooth, about 30 seconds. Divide into custard cups or martini glasses and serve. The pudding will keep in the refrigerator for up to 3 days, with plastic wrap intact.

SERVES 6

HOMEMADE VANILLA BEAN EXTRACT

Why buy vanilla extract when you can make it yourself? Stir 2 cups of vodka with 6 scraped vanilla pods cut into 1-inch lengths. Cover with a tight-fitting lid and set aside for 2 months in a cool, dark spot. Homemade vanilla keeps indefinitely.

Once you've used half the bottle, simply top off with more vodka and set aside until the color becomes rich and amber (this could take a few days). Once the vodka doesn't turn a deep amber color, you know the vanilla beans are spent. Time for a fresh batch!

TAHITIAN VANILLA BEANS

Throughout the book, whenever I call for vanilla beans, I usually specify Tahitian vanilla beans. I find Tahitian vanilla (and even Tahitian vanilla extract) to be a little more floral and softer than the somewhat more grounded Bourbon-style vanilla.

In fact, Tahitian vanilla is actually a different species than Bourbon vanilla (which refers to the former Bourbon Islands, not the whiskey) that is grown in French Polynesia's vanilla archipelago: Taha'a, Raiatea, and Huahine. Vanilla beans are the fruit of a climbing orchid plant originally native to Mexico and shipped by Spanish explorer Hernán Cortés to Europe along with another popular export—cocoa. Vanilla-producing orchids were brought to Tahiti in 1848 and, over the course of half a century, they developed into a new species with more heliotropin, the chemical compound responsible for the sublime perfume of vanilla beans.

Bourbon vanilla has to be harvested before it is fully mature. That's not the case with Tahitian vanilla, which can remain on the vine longer to soak up some rays. Like a tomato or peach that benefits from a few extra days of hot sun, the same is true for vanilla. If you can find Tahitian vanilla beans, definitely try them out—you won't be disappointed.

Banana Pudding
with Vanilla Wafer Crumble

Funerals are a big deal in New Orleans and our family was no exception. Though we didn't send our beloveds off with a jazz funeral and a brass band, we did put out quite a spread to keep the mourners sated. I would sit through the eulogy, the whole time keeping my fingers crossed that I'd meet up with banana pudding at the post-service buffet table at one of the cousin's houses. I'd walk into the gathering and within minutes I'd be scanning the dessert table—nine out of ten times it was there—a giant bowl of canary yellow and banana-flavored righteousness beckoning to be pillaged.

Sometimes it was layered with vanilla wafers like a parfait. Sometimes the cookies were half sunken into the abyss. Sometimes there were bananas and sometimes there weren't. I'd always scoop out a giant serving with more than my fair share of cookies. Now that I'm grown, I like my banana pudding flavored with banana liqueur and topped with a vanilla-wafer and cinnamon-tossed crumb topping. The topping always stays crisp and provides an amazing contrast to the soft-tender bite of the chopped bananas and the silkiness of the pudding. It's humble and homey but just different enough from the traditional version that I feel good about serving it in a more sophisticated setting.

Banana Pudding

FOR THE PUDDING

- 5 large egg yolks
- ½ cup sugar
- ¼ cup cornstarch
- ¼ teaspoon salt
- 2 cups whole milk
- 3 tablespoons banana liqueur (or 1 teaspoon banana flavoring)
- 2 teaspoons vanilla extract
- 2 tablespoons unsalted butter
- 2 ripe bananas

FOR THE CRUMBLE

- 1 cup vanilla wafers (about 15 cookies)
- 2 teaspoons sugar
- ¼ teaspoon ground cinnamon
  Pinch salt
- 1 tablespoon unsalted butter, melted

TO MAKE THE PUDDING

Whisk the egg yolks, sugar, cornstarch, and salt together in a medium bowl and set aside. Bring the milk to a boil in a medium saucepan. Remove from the heat and whisk a little at a time into the egg mixture. Once the bottom of the bowl is warm, slowly whisk in the remaining hot milk. Pour the mixture back into a clean medium saucepan (cleaning the saucepan prevents the pudding from scorching), add the banana liqueur, and whisk over medium-low heat until it thickens, about 2 minutes. Cook while constantly whisking until the pudding is glossy and quite thick, 1½ to 2 minutes longer. Transfer the pudding to a clean bowl.

Add the vanilla and butter and gently whisk until the butter is completely melted and incorporated. Press a piece of plastic wrap onto the surface of the pudding to prevent a skin from forming. Refrigerate for 4 hours.

TO MAKE THE CRUMBLE

While the pudding sets, heat the oven to 325°F. Line a rimmed baking sheet with parchment paper and set aside. Place the wafers in a resealable plastic bag and seal (make sure there is no air in the bag prior to sealing). Using a rolling pin or a flat-bottomed saucepan or pot, crush the vanilla wafers until they're coarsely ground. Transfer them to a small bowl and stir in the sugar, cinnamon, and salt. Use a spoon to evenly stir in the melted butter, transfer to the prepared baking sheet, and toast in the oven until brown and fragrant, 12 to 15 minutes. Remove from the oven and set aside to cool. (The crumbs can be stored in an airtight container for up to 5 days at room temperature or frozen for up to 2 months; re-crisp in a 325°F oven for 6 to 7 minutes if necessary.)

TO SERVE

Slice the bananas in half crosswise and then slice in half lengthwise so you have 4 quarters. Slice the banana quarters crosswise into ½-inch pieces and divide between 6 custard cups or martini glasses (sprinkle with a squeeze of lemon juice if you like—this helps prevent browning). Whisk the pudding until it is soft and smooth, about 30 seconds, and then divide it between the custard cups. Top with the vanilla wafer mixture and serve. (If not served immediately, the pudding will keep in the refrigerator for up to 3 days, with plastic wrap intact. Sprinkle the crumbs on just before serving.)

SERVES 6

Old-Fashioned Chocolate Pudding

Water-skiing on the Tchefuncta River (say it: tche-FUNK-ta) in the summertime was a religion in my family. The day of my christening, my dad, Aunt Boo, and Uncle Donnie (who was her husband) went out for an early morning session and wouldn't you know it, my dad tried to pull off some trick and ended up with a cast on his foot. My christening was cancelled, and Mom has never truly forgiven neither Dad nor Aunt Boo.

As I grew up, I became just as addicted to skiing on the river as they were. Along with my sister, my dad, and my uncle, I'd set out for the river early in the morning, always stopping at Popeye's℠ first to stock up on snacks. Popeye's is a New Orleans franchise, and I remember standing at a window, transfixed by the sight of women stamping out biscuit dough by hand. We'd order up a big box of fried chicken, a whole mess of biscuits, mini pecan pies, and some good old-fashioned chocolate pudding and feast on the whole shebang all day long.

Chocolate pudding is a classic for a reason. I don't mess with it, though I do like to use good-quality semisweet chocolate in addition to a little cocoa powder for an extra deep and rounded chocolatey punch. I also use this pudding as the cake filling in the Doberge cake on p. 60.

Old-Fashioned Chocolate Pudding

5   large egg yolks

½   cup sugar

3   tablespoons cornstarch

2   tablespoons cocoa powder

¼   teaspoon salt

2   cups milk

1   teaspoon vanilla extract

4   ounces semisweet chocolate (preferably 58%–62% cacao), finely chopped

2   tablespoons unsalted butter

Whisk the egg yolks, sugar, cornstarch, cocoa, and salt together in a medium bowl and set aside. Bring the milk to a boil in a medium saucepan. Remove from the heat and whisk a little at a time into the egg mixture. Once the bottom of the bowl is warm, slowly whisk in the remaining hot milk. Pour the mixture back into a clean medium saucepan (cleaning the saucepan prevents the pudding from scorching), add the vanilla, and whisk over medium-low heat until it thickens, 3 to 4 minutes. Cook while constantly whisking until the pudding is glossy and quite thick, 1½ to 2 minutes longer. Transfer the pudding to a clean bowl.

Add the chopped chocolate and the butter and gently whisk until the chocolate is completely incorporated. Press a piece of plastic wrap onto the surface of the pudding to prevent a skin from forming. Refrigerate for 4 hours.

Before serving, whisk the pudding until it is soft and smooth, about 30 seconds. Divide into custard cups or martini glasses and serve. The pudding will keep in the refrigerator for up to 3 days, with plastic wrap intact.

SERVES 6 TO 8

VARIATION

CHOCOLATE CREAM PIE

Fold in 1 cup of medium-stiff whipped cream and spread into the piecrust on p. 44. Top with more whipped cream topping (recipe on p. 45) and some shaved chocolate curls (a vegetable peeler and a block of chocolate create pro-looking curls).

Mahatma Rice Pudding

This rice pudding is about as simple and honest as rice pudding gets. Rice is a major crop in Louisiana (for more information about rice, see "Mahatma Rice and Me" on the facing page), and as such, we Louisianans have conjured up lots of ways to use it. From red beans and rice to fritters and this rice pudding, it's pretty amazing how many ways we can use these humble grains. Cane syrup is a natural finishing touch for me, but maple syrup, molasses, sorghum, or even a handful of brown sugar would be great, too. You can add plumped raisins or a pinch of ground cinnamon if you like. Me, I like to let the flavor of the vanilla bean be the star of the show.

3 cups whole milk

1 cup extra-long-grain white rice (Mahatma brand if you can find it)

⅓ cup sugar

1 vanilla bean

⅛ teaspoon kosher salt

Cane syrup for serving

Place the milk, rice, sugar, vanilla bean, and salt in a medium saucepan over medium-high heat. Bring the mixture to a simmer, stirring often, and then reduce the heat to low, cover, and cook for 15 minutes, stirring every 5 minutes. Turn off the heat, uncover, and stir, and then place the lid back on the pan and let the rice pudding rest for 10 minutes. Serve while warm with a drizzle of cane syrup. (Refrigerated leftovers can be warmed in the microwave with some milk to loosen the pudding.)

SERVES 6

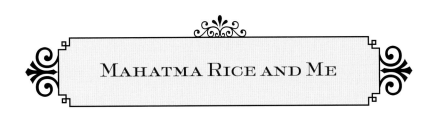

MAHATMA RICE AND ME

I grew up on Mahatma long-grain white rice, a brand that has a huge role in Cajun cuisine from the Acadiana region, in everything from crawfish étouffé to boudin. Though I visited my Aunt Boo in Abbeville often as a kid, I never made the Mahatma-Abbeville connection until I was an adult and actually read the rice package, discovering that Mahatma rice is grown and processed in none other than Aunt Boo's backyard.

Grown in Abbeville, Louisiana, as well as in Arkansas, California, and Texas, Mahatama rice has developed a cult-like following among Cajuns and Creoles for cooking up light and fluffy—I couldn't imagine red beans without it. Introduced in 1932, it's one of the leading long-grain white rice varieties in markets. People are so dedicated to their Mahatma that the company offers its jingle to download for cell phones! For me, keeping a few bags in my cupboard makes me feel like New Orleans isn't so far away.

Café au Lait Crème Brûlée

To get to New Orleans East, where I grew up, from New Orleans, where I went to school, I'd have to drive over the High Rise Bridge (otherwise known as the Industrial Canal Bridge) that reaches over the Industrial Canal, a waterway that connects the Mississippi River to Lake Pontchartrain. The drive was punctuated by the thick, heady smell of coffee beans roasting at the local plant, a fragrance that always reminded me of family, be it "making groceries" at the A&P with Mom and getting our coffee freshly ground at the big red grinder, or having café con leche when visiting Granny, my dad's mom, who probably gave me my first café con leche when I was 7 years old. (My dad, who was born in Havana, drank café con leche as a young boy for breakfast every morning.) Adding coffee to crème brûlée seems like a natural combination to me, bringing my Cuban and New Orleanian heritage together in one incredibly decadent package.

My version of crème brûlée is pretty low maintenance—instead of cooking the custard in a water bath I bake it on a baking sheet at a really low temperature. I find this gives it a silky texture and a nice soft set. Make a modest investment in a hand-held blowtorch (available at most every gourmet cookware shop) or even the big, durable propane tanks from your neighborhood hardware store so you can evenly caramelize the sugar topping quickly, keeping the custard nice and cool. If you have no other option, you can use the broiler to brûlée the sugar, but your custard will warm up a little in the process.

3 tablespoons French roast whole coffee beans

1¼ cups whole milk

1¼ cups heavy cream

6 tablespoons sugar

11 large egg yolks

⅛ teaspoon salt

6 teaspoons demarara sugar

Heat the oven to 200°F. Place the coffee beans in a coffee grinder, pulse for two 1-second pulses (some beans may still be whole, which is okay), and set aside.

Stir the milk, cream, and sugar together in a medium saucepan and bring to a boil over medium-high heat. Turn the heat off, stir in the coffee beans, and let the mixture steep for 5 minutes.

Whisk the egg yolks and salt together in a large bowl. Vigorously whisk the steeped milk mixture into the egg yolks, then strain into a clean bowl. Place six 4-ounce ramekins (preferably shallow oval ramekins, see the equipment note below) on a rimmed baking sheet and evenly divide the custard mixture between them. Place the baking sheet in the oven and bake until a dime-size center portion of the custard gives a slight jiggle when the baking sheet is tapped, about 50 minutes to 1 hour. Let the custards cool at room temperature for 30 minutes before covering each with plastic wrap and refrigerating for at least 8 hours or up to 3 days.

Evenly sprinkle the top of each custard with 1 teaspoon of coarse demarara sugar (if you are using round ramekins, you may not use the full teaspoon) and brown it using a hand-held blowtorch. Serve immediately after brûléeing.

SERVES 6

→EQUIPMENT NOTE I like using shallow, oval-shaped ramekins to make crème brûlée because their long and shallow shape allows for a greater ratio of crisp sugar topping to custard.

100
DEGREES
IN THE SHADE

Ices, Ice Creams & Frozen Confections

A mid-August day in New Orleans simply redefines "hot." Hot, in New Orleans, isn't just the mercury raising its hand above 100°F—it's the humidity that makes the air thicker than cane syrup and the blazing sun that's hotter than beignets fresh out of the fryer. Summer in New Orleans is also when icy syrup-soaked sno-balls and old-fashioned custard-style ice cream taste their best. Luckily, there are plenty of creations that cool New Orleanians from the inside out on sticky summer days. Here are just a few of my favorites for homemade and edible air conditioning.

Lemon-Herbsaint Poppers

These are great served at a cocktail party or a garden party, passed around on a platter with small demitasse spoons. They're bright yellow and taste of citrus with the unmistakable anisey twang of Herbsaint. Herbsaint is a New Orleans creation that debuted right after the repeal of Prohibition (for more information about Herbsaint, see p. 167). Crafted to take the place of outlawed absinthe and imported Pastis, Herbsaint is an essential ingredient in the Sazerac® cocktail, oysters Rockefeller, and my neon yellow poppers.

Lemon-Herbsaint Poppers

2   (0.25-ounce) packages plus 1 teaspoon powdered unflavored gelatin (2 tablespoons total)

½   cup sugar

1   cup club soda

½   cup fresh lemon juice (from 4–6 lemons)

3   tablespoons Herbsaint

Pour ½ cup of cold water into a small bowl, sprinkle the gelatin on top, and set aside.

Bring the sugar and an additional ½ cup of water to a boil in a small saucepan and immediately turn off the heat. Stir the club soda, lemon juice, and Herbsaint together in a medium bowl. Stir the gelatin mixture into the warm sugar water, whisk until dissolved, and then pour into the bowl with the club soda, stirring to combine.

Pour the mixture into an 8-inch-square baking dish or small shot glasses, cover with plastic wrap, and refrigerate until set, about 3 hours or overnight. Set a glass with hot water on your work surface. Dip a paring knife into the hot water and use it to cut the pan of jelled Herbsaint into 1-inch squares. Place a burner on low heat and hold the baking dish over the burner for a split second to release the cubes from the pan. Invert the pan onto a cutting board or platter; the cubes should pop right out (if serving the Herbsaint Poppers in shot glasses, serve as is with a small spoon.) Store the poppers in the refrigerator in an airtight plastic container or in the baking dish covered with plastic wrap for up to 1 week.

SERVES 8

VARIATION

THE SAZERAC—A CLASSIC NEW ORLEANS COCKTAIL IN ALL ITS GLORY
Swirl ½ teaspoon of Herbsaint (or Pernod) inside a rocks glass, making sure it coats the sides. Fill the glass with crushed ice and set aside. In a cocktail shaker half-filled with ice, stir together ¼ cup of bourbon (like Maker's Mark), 1 tablespoon simple syrup (to make: bring ¼ cup water and ¼ cup sugar to a boil, turn off the heat, and cool), 2 to 3 shakes of Peychaud's Bitters, and stir well. Strain into the glass, drop in a lemon twist, and bang it back!

Watermelon Granita–Topped
Sno-Balls

The New Orleans sno-ball is a unique invention of fluffy—not crunchy—flakes of shaved ice that get doused in sweet, flavored syrup. The syrup flavors run the gamut from cherry to nectar cream (see p. 167) and about anything in between. You can get the whole shebang topped with condensed milk or stuffed with soft-serve ice cream (that's how I like it).

There's no way I can even come close to replicating the texture of a sno-ball at home (for that, you'd need a Sno-Bliz® or SnoWizard® machine, a contraption that shaves ice from a block like you would with a handplane). Instead, I've created a kind of granita sno-ball sundae, if you will—sweet watermelon granita on top of a scoop of vanilla ice cream (see p. 110). For the most authentic texture, serve this right after spinning the ice cream in the machine while it's still nice and soft, kind of like the soft serve used to stuff sno-balls.

Watermelon Granita

6 cups diced seedless red watermelon

2 tablespoons fresh lemon juice

2 tablespoons sugar

1 pint vanilla ice cream (or homemade ice cream, p. 110)

Purée the watermelon, lemon juice, and sugar in a blender until liquefied. Pour the mixture into a 9-inch-square glass baking dish and place it on a flat surface in the freezer for 1 hour. Remove the dish from the freezer and use a fork to stir and break the mixture up. Place the dish back in the freezer for another 2 hours or overnight.

Portion the ice cream into 4 bowls. Remove the granita from the freezer. Using a fork, rake the granita from one side of the pan to the other. Cover each serving of ice cream with a quarter of the watermelon granita and serve immediately.

SERVES 4

→MAKE AHEAD While your granita can keep in the freezer for weeks, it has the sweetest, juiciest flavor within 12 hours of being made.

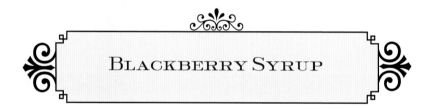

BLACKBERRY SYRUP

This is a beautiful and delicious addition to the granita-topped sno-ball. Follow the first step of the strawberry shortcake recipe on p. 72, substituting blackberries for the strawberries and macerating them for an additional 20 minutes. Strain through a sieve and gently press on the berries to extract as much of the juices as possible. Drizzle over the granita before serving.

SNO-BALLS AND SNOBALLS
(BUT NOT SNOWBALLS)

I can't imagine a New Orleans summer without the promise of a sno-ball at the end of an endlessly hot day. The first sno-ball stand opened in the early 1930s. Proprietors would use a handplane to shave big blocks of ice into fluffy flakes, then pile the flakes into a cup or cone, douse with syrup, and send you on your way. Toward the end of the decade, Ernest Hansen Sr. patented his invention of the Hansen Sno-Bliz, a mechanized (and more sanitary) ice-shaving machine to take the place of shaving ice by hand.

While there are lots of sno-ball (or snoball, as some historians spell it) stands in the city, my two favorites are Hansen's on Tchoupitoulas Street and the Plum Street outfit uptown. Both have been open since the birth of the sno-ball in the '30s. The former is great for homemade syrups and an old-fashioned feel—it's still run by Ernest's granddaughter, Ashley Hansen. Plum Street, also family owned, serves their sno-balls in Chinese-style takeout containers set into a plastic bag (the plastic bag prevents your clothes from getting soiled; if too much water and syrup leak through the container and into the bag, it means you're not eating it fast enough—shame on you!). If you go, you've got to say hi to Donna Black, one of the current owners, who's one of the sweetest proprietors you could hope to meet. The sno-ball season officially begins around Easter time, when the shops open, and continues through early autumn.

Straight Up Vanilla Bean
Ice Cream

❦❦❦❦❦❦❦❦❦❦❦❦❦❦❦❦❦❦❦❦❦

Super rich and very custardy, my vanilla ice cream screams vanilla because I use a real vanilla bean and plenty of egg yolks in the ice cream base. My Uncle Alfred used to churn vanilla ice cream with one of those old-school crank-style machines. The ice cream it yielded was dense and rich, just like a good old-fashioned custard-style ice cream should be. I actually prefer vanilla ice cream made in the hand-crank contraptions to ice cream made in the modern electronic machines—the crank-style machines produce the creamiest ice cream.

If you like your ice cream soft-serve style, scoop it out and eat it right after churning (if you're going to stir cooked fruit, chocolate chips, or nuts into it, now's the time). If you like a hard-set ice cream, repack it in an airtight and freezer-safe container and freeze it for at least a couple of hours before serving. You may need to let it sit out at room temperature for a spell to soften before scooping. Serve on its own, with nectar cream soda (pictured at right) or root beer for a float (see variations, p. 112), on top of the Black & Blue Crumble (p. 48), or with Bananas Foster (p. 10).

❦❦❦❦❦❦❦❦❦❦❦❦❦❦❦❦❦❦❦❦❦

Straight Up Vanilla Bean Ice Cream

1½ cups milk

1½ cups heavy cream

½ cup plus 3 tablespoons sugar

1 vanilla bean (preferably Tahitian, see p. 91), split and scraped, seeds reserved, or 1 teaspoon vanilla extract

8 large egg yolks

Bring the milk, cream, half of the sugar, and the vanilla bean and scraped seeds or extract to a boil in a large pot over medium-high heat. Turn off the heat and set the pot aside. Pour the egg yolks into a large bowl and whisk with the remaining sugar for 30 seconds. Slowly whisk in a little of the hot milk mixture until the bottom of the bowl is warm to the touch. Transfer the egg-milk mixture back into the pot. Cook over low heat, stirring often, until the ice cream base becomes the consistency of eggnog and coats the back of a wooden spoon (use your finger to make a line on the back of the spoon—it should make a clear trail that doesn't run). Once the temperature of the base reaches between 175°F and 180°F on a digital thermometer (after 2½ to 4 minutes), remove from the heat and strain through a coarse-mesh sieve into a clean large bowl.

Fill another large bowl with ice and water (1 part ice to 2 parts water) and set the bowl containing the ice cream base into the water bath (make sure the water doesn't seep into the bowl with the base). Stir the mixture occasionally until it is completely cooled, 45 to 60 minutes, and then refrigerate for at least 4 hours or preferably overnight. Following your ice-cream maker's instructions, churn the cold ice cream base into ice cream. If you like soft serve–style ice cream, then serve and eat right away, or for a hard-style ice cream, transfer the ice cream to a container and place in the freezer until serving.

MAKES 1 QUART

→MAKE AHEAD You can make the ice cream base up to 2 days ahead of churning. Keep it in an airtight container in the refrigerator until you're ready to churn it. And remember that for many ice-cream makers, you need to freeze the container (the part of the machine that you pour the ice cream into) for at least 24 hours before churning the ice cream.

VARIATIONS

NECTAR CREAM SODA FLOAT

Fill a pint glass with ice and add 1 scoop of vanilla ice cream. Pour 2½ tablespoons of nectar syrup (see p. 167) into the glass, top with 2 tablespoons of heavy cream, and then pour in 1¼ cups of club soda or seltzer. Drink immediately, or top with a dollop of chantilly cream (see the recipe on p. 53) before serving.

ABITA ROOT BEER FLOAT

Stack 2 scoops of vanilla ice cream in a pint glass. Pour root beer (preferably Abita brand, though any will do) over the top and serve.

Cane Syrup Ice Cream

This is my south of the Mason-Dixon take on maple ice cream. It's not cloying and is herbal and molasses-like. I totally dig it with brown butter shortcake (p. 70) and Gâteau de Sirop (p. 73). Sometimes when I'm craving it but don't have the time to go through the process of making ice cream, I'll just pour the cane syrup straight over vanilla ice cream. It's so good.

Cane Syrup Ice Cream

2 cups whole milk

2 cups heavy cream

²⁄₃ cup cane syrup

5 large egg yolks

½ teaspoon vanilla extract

¼ teaspoon salt

Bring the milk and cream to a boil in a large pot over medium-high heat. Turn off the heat and set the pot aside. Whisk the cane syrup, egg yolks, vanilla, and salt together in a large bowl, then slowly whisk in a little of the hot milk mixture until the bottom of the bowl is warm to the touch. Transfer the syrupy-milk mixture back into the pot. Cook over low heat, stirring often, until the ice cream base becomes the consistency of eggnog and coats the back of a wooden spoon (use your finger to make a line on the back of the spoon—it should make a clear trail that doesn't run). Once the temperature of the base reaches between 175°F and 180°F on a digital thermometer (after 2½ to 4 minutes), remove from the heat and strain through a fine-mesh sieve into a clean large bowl.

Fill another large bowl with ice and water (1 part ice to 2 parts water) and set the bowl containing the ice cream base into the water bath (make sure the water doesn't seep into the bowl with the base). Stir the mixture occasionally until it is completely cooled, 45 to 60 minutes, and then refrigerate for at least 4 hours or preferably overnight (the ice cream base will keep in the refrigerator for 2 days). Following your ice-cream maker's instructions, churn the cold ice cream base into ice cream. If you like soft serve–style ice cream, then serve and eat right away, or for a hard-style ice cream, transfer the ice cream to a container and place in the freezer until serving.

MAKES 1½ QUARTS

Simply put, cane syrup is to Louisiana what maple syrup is to Vermont. Sweeter and less bitter than molasses, cane syrup has been produced by Steen's since 1910, and the company still adheres to its original recipe: sugar cane is harvested, cut and stripped, and then sent to the mill where the juices are collected and boiled in large open kettles until concentrated into a syrup. Steen's is one of the only traditional cane syrup manufacturers left in the South, and as such, traditional cane syrup has earned a spot on the Slow Food® US Ark of Taste list, a catalog of American food products that are in danger of becoming extinct (also included are Louisiana heritage strawberries, Roman candy, and New Orleans baguettes). Cane syrup can be used in place of molasses, maple syrup, corn syrup, honey, and even granulated sugar—with the latter, reduce the amount of sugar in the recipe by 25% since cane syrup is much sweeter than white sugar.

Pecan & Brown Butter
Ice Cream

When we were craving ice cream, my whole family would pile into the car and head to Angelo Brocato's ice cream and pastry shop on Carrollton Avenue. Family-run for generations, Brocato's is still known for its creamy spumoni and gelato-style ice cream. We all had our favorites—my sister, Tracy, always got chocolate mint chip. Mom and I stayed true to the tiramisu, and Dad always ordered the praline-style ice cream. It took me many years to understand his affection for it, but now I get it completely—sweet, salty, with a caramelly, buttery underpinning, it has become the exception to my "no crunchy stuff in ice cream" rule. In this recipe, I take the butter one step further by browning it on the stovetop first, giving the ice cream a deep, rich, and nutty flavor. Instead of pralines, I use chopped bits of toasted pecans.

1   stick plus 1 tablespoon un-
      salted butter, cut into small
      pieces

1   cup roughly chopped pecans

1½ cups milk

1½ cups heavy cream

½   cup plus 3 tablespoons sugar

8   large egg yolks

Heat the oven to 325°F.

Place the butter in a medium saucepan and melt over medium heat. Simmer the butter, whisking often to incorporate any solids that sink to the bottom of the pan, until it is a golden-amber color and smells nutty, 4 to 6 minutes. The butter should maintain a foam on top filled with tiny bubbles—if it sputters or spatters, reduce the heat. Set the butter aside to cool to room temperature.

Place the pecans on a rimmed baking sheet and roast in the oven until fragrant and toasted, 6 to 8 minutes. Set aside to cool.

Bring the milk, cream, and sugar to a boil in a large pot over medium heat. Turn off the heat and set the pot aside. Place the egg yolks into the bowl of a stand mixer (or into a large bowl if using a hand mixer) and whip on high speed while slowly drizzling in the cooled, browned butter. Once all the butter is added, slowly whisk a little of the hot milk mixture into the egg-butter mixture until the bottom of the bowl is warm to the touch, then add the remaining hot milk. Strain through a fine-mesh sieve into a clean large bowl.

Fill another large bowl with ice and water (1 part ice to 2 parts water) and set the bowl containing the ice cream base into the water bath (make sure the water doesn't seep into the bowl with the base). Stir the mixture occasionally until it is completely cooled, 45 to 60 minutes, and then refrigerate for at least 4 hours or preferably overnight (the ice cream base will keep in the refrigerator for 2 days). Following your ice-cream maker's instructions, churn the cold ice cream base into ice cream. Stir in the toasted pecans. If you like soft serve–style ice cream, then serve and eat right away, or for a hard-style ice cream, transfer the ice cream to a container and place in the freezer until serving.

MAKES 1 QUART

Brandy Milk Punch Ice Cream

Though most New Orleanians might never admit it, I think that many believe that because brandy milk punch has milk in it, it's okay to drink it before noon—heck, even before 10 a.m.! I remember sitting down to special-occasion brunches of eggs sardou (say it: sar-DOUGH) with lots of hollandaise, a side of lyonnaise potatoes, and fried eggplant. The best part was when my mom or dad would hand me their rocks glass filled with brandy milk punch. Though I only was allowed one sweet sip, it was all I needed, giving me just enough to get a feel for the creaminess, the brief flash of fiery brandy, the spice of the nutmeg, and a brandy milk moustache.

1½ cups milk

1½ cups heavy cream

½ cup sugar

6 large egg yolks

2 tablespoons brandy

½ teaspoon vanilla extract

¼ teaspoon freshly grated nutmeg

Bring the milk, cream, and half of the sugar to a boil in a large pot over medium-high heat. Turn off the heat and set the pot aside. Pour the egg yolks into a large bowl and whisk with the remaining sugar for 30 seconds. Slowly whisk in a little of the hot milk mixture until the bottom of the bowl is warm to the touch. Stir in the brandy and vanilla and then pour it back into the pot. Cook over low heat, stirring often, until the ice cream base becomes the consistency of eggnog and coats the back of a wooden spoon (use your finger to make a line on the back of the spoon—it should make a clear trail that doesn't run). Once the temperature of the base reaches between 175°F and 180°F on a digital thermometer (after 2½ to 4 minutes), remove from the heat and strain through a fine-mesh sieve into a clean large bowl.

Fill another large bowl with ice and water (1 part ice to 2 parts water) and set the bowl containing the ice cream base into the water bath (make sure the water doesn't seep into the bowl with the base). Add the nutmeg and stir the mixture occasionally until it is completely cooled, 45 to 60 minutes, and then refrigerate for at least 4 hours or preferably overnight. Following your ice-cream maker's instructions, churn the cold ice cream base into ice cream. If you like soft serve–style ice cream, then serve and eat right away, or for a hard-style ice cream, transfer the ice cream to a container and place in the freezer until serving.

MAKES 1 QUART

EYE OPENERS

Brunch in New Orleans is sacred. It's all about eggs, a quarter-pound of jumbo lump crab meat, and buttery hollandaise—all accompanied by a spiked libation on the side, like a Sazerac (p. 106), a Ramos gin fizz, an absinthe frappe, or brandy milk punch. These are the cocktails to order in the land where many believe the cocktail was invented. As a prelude to even a morning coffee, eye openers are said to help cure hangovers and get you in the right frame of mind to tackle—or succumb to—the day.

SPREADABLE
SWEETS

Curds, Jams & Preserves

Nanny, my great-aunt on Aunt Boo's side of the family, was the jam and jelly maker. Nanny's garage was stockpiled with a Technicolor® array of jams, jellies, and preserves from mayhaw (a fruit that grows on hawthorn trees) to strawberry and more. Canning and preserving is a real southern thing, with people pickling and jamming year-round to capture the flavor of the season's best fresh fruits and vegetables and preserving enough of it to get through to the next season. There's nothing like pulling out a jar of peak-season strawberry jam in the dead of winter, popping the top, and slathering it on a biscuit or toast. The recipes in this chapter offer a fruit to put up for nearly every season, from late winter and spring's sweetest strawberries (the season actually peaks in February in Louisiana) to summer blueberries, fall figs, and winter lemons.

Hammond-Independence
Blueberry Jam

After the strawberry season ends, Louisianans start pining for the berries that come from the Hammond and Independence areas, not far from where I used to go with my family on a post-Thanksgiving retreat called the "Gathering of the Greens." We'd pick pine needles and boughs to make holiday wreaths and all gather around long picnic tables to shell (and eat) pecans that would inevitably turn into pecan pie. In any case, Hammond and Independence are only about 1½ hours north of New Orleans, making the route from farm to market a short one, meaning the berries get picked at their pinnacle of perfection and trucked down to the city so berry lovers can get them while the gettin's good.

Hammond-Independence Blueberry Jam

1¼ pounds blueberries

3 cups sugar

Zest of 1 lemon

1½ teaspoons pectin

Place a small ceramic or glass plate in the freezer. Place the blueberries in a large bowl and mash with 2¾ cups of the sugar and the lemon zest. Transfer the mixture to a medium saucepan and cook over medium heat until the juices simmer, 3 to 4 minutes, stirring often.

Meanwhile, mix the pectin with the remaining ¼ cup of sugar. Add the pectin mixture to the blueberries and continue to cook until the mixture reaches 220°F to 222°F, another 30 to 35 minutes (note that the jam will stay at around 217°F for what seems like an eternity—be patient, the temperature will rise, so stick with it), skimming the foam from the top and stirring every so often. Take the plate out of the freezer and spoon a small dollop of jam onto it. The jam should set up semi-stiff, and when you run your finger through it, the trail should not run back together immediately. If it does, keep cooking. If it doesn't, turn off the heat and let the jam sit for 10 minutes. (This helps ensure that your berries don't float to the top of the jam jar.)

→ TIP While you don't have to skim your jam, it does make for a beautifully clear suspension. I think it's worth the effort.

Fill a large stockpot or canning pot with water and bring to a boil. Add the jars, lids, and bands, and simmer for 5 minutes. Use tongs to remove the jars, bands, and lids to a clean kitchen towel. Once cool enough to handle (but still warm) fill the jars nearly full with blueberry jam, leaving a ½-inch space at the top. Screw the lids on.

Add more water to the pot if necessary and bring to a boil. Place a canning rack in the pot and set the filled jars into the rack. Boil the jars for 10 minutes (the filled jars should be completely covered by the boiling water). Using tongs, remove the jars and place on the kitchen towel. If refrigerating, be sure to cool the filled jars for at least a few hours first. Unopened, the jam will keep in a cool, dark place for a few months. After opening, try to eat the jam within a week or two (not that it will last that long!).

MAKES FIVE 8-OUNCE JARS

Ponchatoula Strawberry Jam

I don't make this jam until strawberry season rolls around. In Louisiana it runs from as early as late December through the beginning of April, and that's when the best strawberries hit the farm stands. While southern jam is all about being sweet—and I don't mean just sweet, I mean eye-squinting sweet—in this version, I curb the sugar a bit, because I don't want to mask the strawberry's delicate floral qualities with a ton of sugar.

I have to give a shout-out to Lucy Mike, the Strawberry Ambassador of Ponchatoula. She hooked me up with some farm-fresh berries one season and I've got to say, they made the best darn strawberry jam I've ever had. If you ever get the opportunity to buy some real Ponchatoula berries, you've just got to try them in this jam.

Ponchatoula Strawberry Jam

2½ pounds strawberries, hulled, small and medium strawberries left whole and large ones quartered

3¼ cups sugar

Zest of 1 lemon

1½ teaspoons pectin

Place a small ceramic or glass plate in the freezer. Place the strawberries, 3 cups of the sugar, and the lemon zest in a large pot over medium heat. Cook, stirring occasionally, folding the strawberries and sugar together until the sugar is dissolved and the mixture comes to a simmer, about 10 minutes.

Meanwhile, mix the pectin with the remaining ¼ cup of sugar. Add the pectin mixture to the strawberries and continue to cook until the mixture reaches 220°F to 222°F, another 30 to 35 minutes (note that the jam will stay at around 217°F for what seems like an eternity—be patient, the temperature will rise, so stick with it), skimming the foam from the top and stirring every so often. Take the plate out of the freezer and spoon a small dollop of jam onto it. The jam should set up semi-stiff, and when you run your finger through it, the trail should not run back together immediately. If it does, keep cooking. If it doesn't, turn off the heat and let the jam sit for 10 minutes. (This helps ensure that your berries don't float to the top of the jam jar.)

Fill a large stockpot or canning pot with water and bring to a boil. Add the jars, lids, and bands, and simmer for 10 minutes. Use tongs to remove the jars, bands, and lids to a clean kitchen towel. Once cool enough to handle (but still warm) fill the jars nearly full with strawberry jam, leaving a ½-inch space at the top. Screw the lids on.

Add more water to the pot if necessary and bring to a boil. Place a canning rack in the pot and set the filled jars into the rack. Boil the jars for 10 minutes (the filled jars should be completely covered by the boiling water). Using tongs, remove the jars and place on the kitchen towel. If refrigerating, be sure to cool the filled jars for a few hours first. Unopened, the jam will keep in a cool, dark place for a few months. After opening, try to eat the jam within a week or two.

MAKES FIVE 8-OUNCE JARS

→TIP Try to go for smaller strawberries rather than larger ones. Smaller berries stay whole and suspended within the jam like little jewels, but when you go to spread it, the strawberries completely disintegrate and schmear like butter. If you can't get small berries, just halve or quarter the big guys.

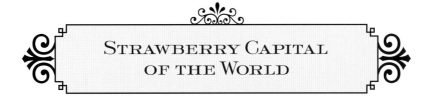

STRAWBERRY CAPITAL OF THE WORLD

Louisiana grows its finest, sweetest, and most delicious strawberries in the town of Ponchatoula, about 1 hour north of New Orleans and officially known as the "Strawberry Capital of the World." People say, and I concur, that the soil and sun of Louisiana make for more tender and sweeter berries than those grown in California and Florida.

For the people of Ponchatoula, the strawberry industry has been an important facet of life for more than 100 years, celebrated every year in early April at the Ponchatoula Strawberry Festival. At the festival, an estimated 300,000 strawberry die-hards descend on the town to live, breathe, and feast on strawberry pastries, shortcakes, and the obligatory seafood gumbo and fried alligator thrown in for good measure. Add a baking contest, a parade (with a Strawberry King and Queen, of course), music, and rides, and you've got one heck of a party.

In the early 1900s, the invention of the refrigerated railcar and a new strain of strawberry plant that yielded large, sturdy berries converged with the expansion of the New Orleans-Chicago railroad line, propelling Ponchatoula into the big leagues of the strawberry business. During the Depression and after the closure of several lumber mills, the people of Ponchatoula became even more reliant on strawberry farming as a way to support their families. As such, the industry peaked during the 1930s; after the boys came home from World War II and started working in chemical and industrial plants rather than the strawberry fields, the industry suffered.

While Ponchatoula led the state in strawberry growing, it wasn't known as the strawberry capital (that title belonged to Hammond, 6 miles north of Ponchatoula) until 1968. In 2001, the strawberry replaced the cantaloupe as Louisiana's official state fruit.

The number of strawberry growers in Louisiana has become fewer and fewer, with only an estimated 300 to 400 acres currently devoted to strawberry growing (that's as much as one giant California strawberry farm). As a result, Slow Food USA has declared Louisiana heritage strawberries like the Daybreak, Headliner, Klondike, and Tangi as a part of its Ark of Taste project, an effort to document unique food items and cultivate demand, thereby saving heritage foods from disappearing forever from our plates.

Lemon Curd

This lemon curd is really special. Unlike lemon curds you may have made in the past, which can be gelatinous and dense, this one is incredibly light, creamy, buttery, and a beautiful shade of pale yellow. The secret is in how the butter is incorporated. I add in the butter using a food processor so it emulsifies—it's the coolest thing, almost magical, really. It sets up pudding-like, with an amazing satiny texture and out-of-this-world flavor. It's a very un-southern way of making a very southern dish. Thanks to Jason Andelman, a local chocolatier in Arlington, Virginia, for showing me this trick so I could pass it on to you.

This lemon curd is wonderful solo or topped with the vanilla wafer crumble on p. 94 (crushed gingersnaps work, too). For lemon pie, simply use the curd as a filling for a graham cracker crust (like the one on p. 53) or piecrust (p. 44).

4–6 lemons

6 large eggs

1½ cups sugar

2 sticks unsalted butter, at room temperature, each stick quartered

Grate the zest from 2 of the lemons and place in a medium heatproof bowl. Juice enough lemons to yield 1 cup of lemon juice and add to the zest along with the eggs and sugar. Bring a medium saucepan filled with water to a depth of 1 inch to a simmer over medium-high heat. Place the bowl with the egg mixture over the saucepan, reduce the heat to low, and whisk the mixture vigorously every 5 minutes until thick, about 20 minutes.

Use a rubber spatula to transfer the curd to a food processor. With the machine running, add the butter one piece at a time, processing for 10 to 15 seconds between additions and making sure that the butter is incorporated before adding the next portion. Process the lemon curd until all of the butter is added and the curd is completely smooth. Scrape down the sides of the bowl and blend for another 15 seconds.

Divide the hot curd evenly between four 8-ounce jars or a plastic container. Lay plastic wrap directly on top of the curd's surface and cover with a lid. Refrigerate for up to 5 days or freeze for up to 3 months.

MAKES 1 QUART, ENOUGH FOR FOUR 8-OUNCE MASON JARS

Fig Jam

The Hingles lived across the street from my house in New Orleans East. They were thoughtful neighbors, always waving when we pulled into our driveway and paying me to cut their lawn. After a fruitful day on Lake Pontchartrain, Mr. Hingle would bring over some shrimp or speckled trout that he had caught for my mom to cook up. Mrs. Hingle was generous with her bounty, too—in the fall, when the branches on their mission fig tree bowed down with fruit, Mrs. Hingle would stop over with a few baskets brimming with the plump figs. Eating fig jam with my two boys, Spencer and Kemp, always brings me back to being 16, mowing the lawn on gorgeous autumn days, and to the taste of the Hingles' jammy-sweet figs.

Fig Jam

¾ cup sugar

1½ teaspoons pectin

3 pounds black mission figs

2 tablespoons lemon juice (preferably freshly squeezed)

2 tablespoons honey (preferably a dark amber honey like sourwood or basswood)

→TIP I like my jams on the loose side. If you prefer a tighter, more solid jam, let it simmer a few minutes longer on the stovetop so the juices can further cook down.

Place a small ceramic or glass plate in the freezer. Stir ½ cup of the sugar with the pectin in a small bowl and set aside. Combine the remaining ¼ cup of sugar with the figs, lemon juice, and honey in a large heavy-bottomed pot. Cook over medium heat, stirring occasionally, until it comes to a simmer, 5 to 6 minutes. Whisk in the sugar-pectin mixture and reduce the heat to medium-low. Use a wooden spoon to gently mash the figs and break them apart (you want a rough mixture, not mush), and continue to cook, stirring occasionally, until the mixture reaches 212°F, 8 to 10 minutes. Skim off any foam from the mixture.

Take the plate out of the freezer and spoon a small dollop of jam onto it. The jam should set up semi-stiff, and when you run your finger through it, the trail should not run back together immediately. If it does, keep cooking. If it doesn't, turn off the heat and let the figs sit for 10 minutes (this helps ensure that your fruit doesn't float to the top of the jam jar).

Fill a large stockpot or canning pot with water and bring to a boil. Add the jars, lids, and bands, and simmer for 5 minutes. Use tongs to remove the jars, bands, and lids to a clean kitchen towel. Once cool enough to handle (but still warm) fill the jars nearly full with fig jam, leaving a ½-inch space at the top. Screw the lids on.

Add more water to the pot if necessary and bring to a boil. Place a canning rack in the pot and set the filled jars into the rack. Boil the jars for 10 minutes (the filled jars should be completely covered by the boiling water). Using tongs, remove the jars and place on the kitchen towel. If refrigerating, be sure to cool the filled jars a few hours first. Unopened, the jam will keep for a few months. After opening, try to eat the jam within a week or two.

MAKES SIX 8-OUNCE JARS

Honey-Poached Kumquats

❧❧❧❧❧❧❧❧❧❧❧❧❧❧❧❧❧❧❧❧❧

I had already decided to include this recipe in *DamGoodSweet* when I heard the news that Aunt Boo had lost her kumquat tree to Hurricane Rita. When I was a kid, if I wasn't using Aunt Boo's kumquats for slingshots, I was eating them straight from that tree. They were borderline unbearably sour, but something about the kumquat's unmistakable sweet-astringent flavor always made me reach out to pick another one. Then I figured out that the fruit was sour and the rind sweet, so I started eating kumquats like corn-on-the-cob, nibbling off the rind and discarding the fruit.

As I got going with my career in pastry, I rediscovered kumquats. They've since become one of my favorite citruses to play around with. I love to poach them with honey and vanilla beans, or turn them into preserves for spooning on hot biscuits or serving with cake. These poached kumquats are killer over chocolate ice cream or with chocolate cupped cakes (p. 80).

❧❧❧❧❧❧❧❧❧❧❧❧❧❧❧❧❧❧❧❧❧

Honey-Poached Kumquats

2 pints kumquats, quartered lengthwise

½ cup light corn syrup

¼ cup honey

1 cup orange juice (preferably freshly squeezed)

1 vanilla bean, split down the middle, seeds scraped from the pod and reserved

Use the tip of a paring knife to remove any visible seeds from the kumquat quarters and set the quarters aside. Bring 1 cup of water, the corn syrup, honey, orange juice, and vanilla bean and scraped seeds to a boil in a medium saucepan. Add the kumquats, reduce the heat to medium-low, and simmer gently for 30 minutes. Turn off the heat and let the kumquats cool in the poaching liquid. Transfer the kumquats and the poaching liquid to an airtight container and refrigerate for up to a couple of weeks.

To can, fill a large stockpot or canning pot with water and bring to a boil. Add the jars, lids, and bands, and simmer for 10 minutes. Use tongs to remove the jars, bands, and lids to a clean kitchen towel. Once cool enough to handle (but still warm) fill the jars nearly full with the kumquats and poaching liquid, leaving a ½-inch space at the top. Screw the lids on.

Add more water to the pot if necessary and bring to a boil. Place a canning rack in the pot and set the filled jars into the rack. Boil the jars for 10 minutes (the filled jars should be completely covered by the boiling water). Using tongs, remove the jars and place on the kitchen towel. If refrigerating, be sure to cool the filled jars for a few hours first. Unopened, the kumquats will keep in a cool, dark place for a few months. After opening, try to eat the kumquats within a week or two.

MAKES ABOUT 3 PINTS

Red Pepper Jelly

Whether you live in the Garden District or Plaquemines Parish (say it: PLAQUE-uh-mines PEAR-ish), pepper jelly with cream cheese and Triscuits® makes an appearance at every party buffet table in New Orleans. I like it with cream cheese on my biscuits for breakfast, too (see the recipe on p. 137). If you can find long and slender red peppers (they kind of look like deep red Cubanelle or banana peppers), use them. If not, red bell peppers work fine—use one medium to large one to replace the two smaller red peppers.

Red Pepper Jelly

5   large or 6 medium jalapeños

2   medium-size sweet red peppers, stemmed, seeded, veined, and roughly chopped

½   sweet onion (like a Vidalia or Maui), roughly chopped

1½   cups cider vinegar

4   cups sugar

2   teaspoons pectin

Stem, seed, vein, and roughly chop the jalapeños (if they taste mild, you can reserve some seeds and veins to add to the jelly) and set aside. Place a small ceramic or glass plate in the freezer. Purée the jalapeños, red peppers, onions, and ½ cup of the vinegar in a food processor, stopping to scrape down the sides with a rubber spatula once or twice to ensure a fine mixture.

Stir ½ cup of sugar with the pectin in a small bowl and set aside. Combine the remaining 3½ cups of sugar with the puréed peppers in a large heavy-bottomed pot. Cook over medium heat, stirring occasionally, until it comes to a simmer, 5 to 6 minutes. Whisk in the sugar-pectin mixture, reduce the heat to medium-low, and continue to cook, stirring occasionally, until the mixture reaches 220°F to 222°F, 8 to 10 minutes. Skim the orange foam from the mixture.

Take the plate out of the freezer and spoon a small dollop of jelly onto it. The jelly should set up semi-stiff, and when you run your finger through it, the trail should not run back together immediately. If it does, keep cooking. If it doesn't, turn off the heat and let the jelly sit for 10 minutes.

Fill a large stockpot or canning pot with water and bring to a boil. Add the jars, lids, and bands, and simmer for 5 minutes. Use tongs to remove the jars, bands, and lids to a clean kitchen towel. Once cool enough to handle (but still warm) fill the jars nearly full with the pepper jelly, leaving a ½-inch space at the top. Screw the lids on.

Add more water to the pot if necessary and bring to a boil. Place a canning rack in the pot and set the filled jars into the rack. Boil the jars for 10 minutes (the filled jars should be completely covered by the boiling water). Using tongs, remove the jars and place on the kitchen towel. If refrigerating, be sure to cool the filled jars for a few hours first. Unopened, the jelly will keep in a cool, dark place for a few months. After opening, try to eat the jelly within a week or two.

MAKES FOUR 8-OUNCE JARS

→TIP Jalapeños vary in their heat—sometimes you get a batch that's incendiary, sometimes you pick a few as mild as a green bell pepper. That's why it's always a good idea to taste a super thin slice before using them. If it tastes mild, feel free to add some seeds and membranes to the food processor when puréeing the jalapeños with the other ingredients. On the flip side, if it's wicked hot, seed and stem the pepper and only use the pepper meat.

Proper Southern Biscuits
with Pepper Jelly & Cream Cheese

Biscuits are a staple with your pepper jelly, used instead of the brown butter cake for a strawberry shortcake (see the recipe on p. 70), with butter and Steen's, or beneath a heap of smothered onions. Low-protein White Lily® flour is the key to my tender, fluffy biscuits. See p. 166 for information and sources. I like to mix my biscuits by hand, working the liquid into the dry with my fingers. Think about it—it's like using a five-pronged spoon. Your fingers work the liquid into the dough quicker than a wooden spoon, yielding a less-stressed dough (and more tender biscuits).

FOR THE BISCUITS

2¼ cups White Lily flour (not self-rising)

2 tablespoons baking powder

¾ teaspoon salt

1 stick cold unsalted butter, cut into ½-inch pieces, plus 2 tablespoons, melted

1 cup buttermilk

FOR THE CREAM CHEESE

8 ounces cream cheese, cut in half (save half for another time)

½–¾ cup Red Pepper Jelly (facing page)

Heat the oven to 400°F. Line a baking sheet with parchment paper and set aside.

Place 2 cups of the flour, the baking powder, and salt in a food processor and pulse to combine. Add the cold butter pieces and process for ten 1-second pulses (there shouldn't be any pieces of butter bigger than a small pea). Transfer the mixture to a large bowl and begin adding ¾ cup of the buttermilk, incorporating it into the dry ingredients by moving your hand around in circles. Stop adding buttermilk when a dough just barely forms.

Dust your work surface with the remaining ¼ cup of flour and place the dough on top. Roll the dough to a 1-inch thickness. Using a round biscuit cutter 2¼ inches in diameter, punch out as many biscuits as you can and place them on the parchment paper. Gently bring the dough scraps together into a block and press to a 1-inch thickness. Punch out a few more biscuits, place them on the baking sheet, and discard any remaining scraps.

Brush the tops of the biscuits with the remaining buttermilk and bake until golden brown, 20 to 25 minutes. Remove from the oven and brush with the melted butter. Place the cream cheese in a shallow dish or on a small wood block. Spoon the pepper jelly over the top and serve with the warm biscuits.

MAKES ABOUT 10 BISCUITS

→MAKE AHEAD Biscuits are best eaten within a few hours of baking. If you have leftover biscuits, store them in an airtight container or a zip-top bag. Day-after biscuits are great split, lightly toasted, and spread with some good jam.

Lagniappes

Little Somethings & Sweet Send-Offs

Lagniappe (say it: LAN-yap). The word rolls off my tongue and always has. I grew up with lagniappes, the little something extra you get, be it at the end of a meal, as a gift from a host, from a chef, at a bar, wherever. I never realized that the rest of the country didn't know what a lagniappe was until I went to Colorado for college—and then I found out right quick that lagniappes, along with neutral grounds (median strips) and makin' groceries (grocery shopping), were part of a New Orleanian's lexicon and no one else's. I had to leave New Orleans to appreciate what I had there, and I feel so fortunate to have grown up with these incredibly rich traditions. New Orleans will always have a special place in my heart and stomach. Through this cookbook, I hope to pass on the culture to my two sons and to everyone who reads it and cooks from it.

Heavenly Hash

Heavenly hash is like a rocky road candy bar—it's a fudgy, chewy, and unbelievably delicious chocolate confection made with pecans and marshmallows. Locals say that it's so sugar-sweet it'll send you on a sugar high straight to the Pearly Gates. Popularized by New Orleans' family-owned Elmer Candy Company, the egg-shaped sweets were a part of my Easter basket tradition growing up (they always remind me of holiday shopping with my mom at Maison Blanche on Canal Street), and now I make homemade heavenly hash squares for my kids. Heavenly hash is pretty easy to make and is a great hostess gift. Wrap the small squares in decorative foil or place in candy cups for a finished presentation.

Heavenly Hash

1 cup sugar

1 cup evaporated milk

2 tablepoons light corn syrup

¾ pound semisweet chocolate (preferably 58%–61% cacao), finely chopped

1 teaspoon vanilla extract

¼ teaspoon salt

1½ cups toasted pecan pieces

1½ cups mini marshmallows

Lightly coat an 8-inch-square baking dish with nonstick cooking spray. Place a 10-inch-square piece of parchment paper in the baking dish, coat with nonstick cooking spray, and set the dish aside.

Bring the sugar, evaporated milk, and corn syrup to a boil in a medium saucepan over medium-high heat, stirring occasionally. Reduce the heat to medium and simmer until the syrup reaches 220°F (it will have a foam of finely textured bubbles on top like the foam on a beer), about 8 minutes.

Turn off the heat and whisk in the chocolate, vanilla, and salt until the chocolate is completely melted and the mixture is smooth. Let it cool for 3 minutes (you shouldn't feel any heat if you touch a dab to the bottom of your lip) and then stir in the pecans and marshmallows until combined.

Transfer the mixture to the prepared baking sheet and spread it into a somewhat even layer using a rubber spatula (it's okay if it's a little bumpy and rustic). Tap the pan on your work surface a couple of times to compact, and then cover flush with plastic wrap and refrigerate for at least 1 hour or overnight.

Place a deep bowl or pitcher of hot water next to your work surface. Invert the chocolate onto a cutting board and carefully remove the parchment paper. Dip a chef's knife or pizza wheel into the hot water and cut the bar into 2-inch squares. Place the heavenly hash in paper candy cups, wrap in decorative foil, or arrange on a serving platter and refrigerate. Let the candies sit out at room temperature for at least 30 minutes before serving.

MAKES 16 SQUARES

→MAKE AHEAD Heavenly hash keeps for up to 5 days in the refrigerator. Note that the older it gets, the softer the nuts will become.

Pralines

(Say it: Prah-LEENS)

A trip to the French Market on Decatur Street always turned into a special occasion once we sat down at Café du Monde for beignets. After gobbling them up and leaving only traces of powdered sugar behind (because I'd end up wearing most of it!), I'd wander down the river side of the market to Aunt Sally's Praline Shop, where the smell of caramelizing sugar and pecans lured me into the store. Aunt Sally's pralines are still traditionally made by hand just like they were 25 years ago, in small batches and in an old copper pot over a gas stove. When I was a kid I'd press my nose up against the viewing window and watch the pralines get stirred and scooped out from the pot and onto marble slabs to cool and get bagged.

Pralines are best eaten fresh-made when they're still melt-in-your-mouth creamy and tender. After about 3 days, the sugars may start to crystallize and the pralines can potentially lose that amazing tenderness and become more brittle. Once this happens, I like to crumble them over ice cream or grind them into flour for a fruit-crisp topping.

Pralines

4 tablespoons unsalted butter

½ cup plus 4 tablespoons heavy cream

1 cup sugar

1¼ cups packed light brown sugar

2 cups pecan pieces

Line two rimmed baking sheets with parchment paper and set aside.

Melt the butter in a medium saucepan over medium-low heat. Stir in the ½ cup of cream and both sugars until they are dissolved. Increase the heat to medium and simmer until the mixture reaches 240°F to 250°F, using a heatproof rubber spatula to gently push the mixture back and forth in the middle and around the edges occasionally. (If the mixture begins to crystallize, add 2 tablespoons of the cream and continue to cook until it loosens up.)

Stir in the pecans, turn off the heat, and give the mixture a final gentle stir, making sure to get into the bottom and corners of the pan. Using a wooden spoon, portion about 2 tablespoons of the praline mixture onto the prepared baking sheets, leaving at least 1 inch between each praline. Usually by the time I portion out about half of the mixture, what's left in the pan begins to crystallize and stiffen. When this happens, add the last 2 tablespoons of cream and place the saucepan back onto medium heat until the mixture looks creamy and saucy, and then continue portioning out the rest of the pralines. Cool for 30 minutes and then transfer to an airtight container. Pralines stored properly last for up to 3 days before they begin to crystallize.

MAKES ABOUT 3 DOZEN

VARIATIONS

CHOCOLATE PRALINES
Gently stir ½ cup of chopped bittersweet chocolate (preferably 66%–72% cacao) into the mixture when you add the pecans.

COFFEE & CHICORY PRALINES
Bring ½ cup plus 2 tablespoons of heavy cream and 2 tablespoons of ground coffee and chicory (preferably Community Coffee, French Market® coffee, or Café du Monde® brands) to a boil. Turn off the heat and steep for 5 minutes, then strain through a fine-mesh sieve and set aside. Proceed with the praline recipe above, using the coffee-infused cream in place of plain heavy cream.

According to legend, sugar-coated almonds called pralines were invented in the 1700s by the chef to the Duke of Plessis-Praslin, a French marshal and diplomat, to cure his indigestion. I don't know if they did the trick, but the sugary-nutty confections were a hit on the Continent and began to gain popularity in France and Belgium.

Now the story goes like this: A New Orleanian gentleman was visiting Paris on business, ate a praline, and fell in love with it. He brought some home and asked his head cook to replicate them. Instead of making them with almonds, the cook made the pralines with native Louisiana pecans and that was that —the praline (say it: prah-LEEN, not PRAY-leen) was born. By the mid-1800s, Creole women called pralinères lined the streets of the city, selling individual candies from baskets. Nowadays, most pralines are sold in small boutiques and gift shops, like Aunt Sally's on Decatur Street or Pralines by Jean on St. Charles Avenue, though the best ones are always homemade.

IF YOU DON'T HAVE A DIGITAL THERMOMETER

elieve it or not, pralines were made before the invention of digital thermometers, so if you don't have one, don't worry. Just test the sugar mixture this way: After cooking for about 4 minutes, drop a small bit of the sugar (without pecans) into a bowl of ice water. You should be able to form the sugar into a soft, malleable ball in the water—this is called "soft ball" stage. If the sugar forms into a hard ball, then it's too hot and needs to cool before portioning out the pralines. If the sugar doesn't form a ball at all, then it needs to cook a little longer.

Roman Chewing Candy

The Eastern Seaboard has saltwater taffy and New Orleans has Roman candy. As a kid, the Roman candy man was my Good Humor® guy—I was an expert at spotting his mule-drawn carriage from like a half-mile away. I'd kick the back of my mom's seat until she pulled the car over, and that was that! To this day, the Roman candy man still parks his carriage on St. Charles near Napoleon, and to this day, the candy only comes in three flavors: chocolate, vanilla, and strawberry. I remember being mesmerized watching the candy man make it right there in a copper pot on a burner, stretching and wrapping it around a giant taffy hook, and then cutting, rolling, and wrapping it in waxed paper. For me, Roman candy is up there with sno-balls as something that makes New Orleans so unique and special.

Whenever I'm visiting the city with my boys, we always try to search out the Roman candy man. I see the excitement in their eyes, and it makes me feel all warm inside, knowing that I have passed this wonderful tradition on to them. This is not a quick and easy candy to make. It takes some patience and practice, but the end results are worth it, especially if you, like me, grew up eating Roman candy. It's the only way to travel back in time that I know of.

You're going to need rubber gloves and a slab of granite marble to make taffy. It's also best made on cool days. If it's hot and humid, save yourself the trouble and make it another time.

Roman Chewing Candy

2 tablespoons unsalted butter, at room temperature

1 cup light corn syrup

½ cup sugar

1½ teaspoons cider vinegar

¼ teaspoon salt

½ teaspoon vanilla extract (or chocolate or strawberry extract)

Grease a large granite or marble cutting board or work surface with 1 tablespoon of the butter and set aside.

Place the corn syrup, sugar, cider vinegar, 2 teaspoons of the butter, and the salt in a small heavy-bottomed saucepan over medium heat. Place the cover on slightly askew and bring to a simmer, stirring occasionally, for 3 minutes (be careful not to splash too much syrup on the sides of the pan so the mixture doesn't crystallize). Remove the cover and continue to simmer until the syrup reaches 250°F on a digital thermometer, about 5 minutes (start watching the mixture closely at 246°F—the temperature will climb to 250°F really fast). Remove from the heat and stir in the extract.

Pour the hot mixture onto the prepared work surface and let it sit untouched for 1 minute. Grease a metal bench scraper or metal spatula with a little of the remaining butter (about ½ teaspoon) so the taffy doesn't stick to it and begin to fold the sugar from the outer edges into the center, folding the mixture onto itself until it is cool enough to handle (but still flexible enough to stretch easily).

Put on a pair of rubber gloves and grease them with the rest of the remaining butter. Pick up the taffy, holding one end in each hand, and stretch it out by simultaneously and steadily swinging your arms out to your sides. Keep stretching until the taffy is shiny, anywhere from 3 to 5 minutes. Pinch off a small piece and put it on your work surface—it should hold its shape when set down. If it doesn't, continue to stretch the taffy until a small piece holds its shape.

Use scissors to snip the stretched taffy into 6 pieces. Roll each piece into a long, tapered candle-shaped rope about 12 inches long and ½ inch thick. Cut six 12-inch-long by 4-inch pieces of waxed paper and roll each piece of taffy in it, twisting the ends to seal. Store the taffy in an airtight container for up to 3 days.

MAKES 6 PIECES

A New Orleans Legend:
The Roman Candy Man

It's easy to take certain things for granted in New Orleans—like there will always be beignets to order at Café du Monde, and in August, it will be hotter and stickier than caramel coming straight out of a pan. But there's one thing, one guy actually, who I don't take for granted—Ron Kotteman, also known as the Roman Candy Man.

Ron's grandfather, Sam Cortese, came from Siciliy. He hawked fruits and vegetables from a wagon in the summertime and sold firewood in the winter. In 1915, he decided to start selling his mother's candy, a taffy-like confection they christened Roman candy. The taffy was made

and hand pulled in a mule-drawn cart that Sam designed himself. He stretched the taffy into foot-long sticks and then rolled it in waxed paper. He'd drive the cart around the city, parking it along the wide boulevards. It was a hit almost instantly.

Ron started helping his grandfather with the Roman candy business when he was just 14 years old. In 1971, he took over the business and has been hand-pulling chocolate-, strawberry-, and vanilla-flavored taffy ever since. Even though his long-time mule and compatriot, Patsy, sadly passed on in the fall of 2008, Ron continues to pull the original candy cart around town with a pick-up truck (at the time this book went to press, he still hadn't found a replacement for Patsy), most often along St. Charles Avenue in the Garden District.

The candy man cart is an old-school tradition, dating back nearly a hundred years. I almost expect that every time I come home to New Orleans, I'll hear that Ron has retired and the days of the roving candy man are over. Whenever I see his cart pulled to the curb or hear him ringing his bell to let people know he's there, I breathe a huge sigh of relief. Then I pull over and buy one of each flavor.

Spiced Pecans

These spiced pecans are not only fantastic with an Abita root beer, but they're great on cheese boards, in salads (especially with blue cheese), on top of sweet potatoes with brown sugar and butter, and served alongside cocktails. Warming spices like cinnamon and nutmeg combine with the brown sugar to give the pecans that addictive sweetness, while a splash of Crystal's hot sauce (pecans plus hot sauce—a true Louisiana marriage!) and a bit of cayenne add tongue-tingling heat. The combination is so unbelievable that I often find myself baking and bagging these nuts to give as gifts instead of cookies during the holidays.

2   large egg whites

⅓   cup light brown sugar

1   teaspoon hot sauce (prefer-
     ably Crystal's)

½   teaspoon ground cinnamon

½   teaspoon freshly grated
     nutmeg

¼   teaspoon cayenne

½   teaspoon salt

¼   teaspoon freshly ground
     black pepper

4   cups pecan halves

Heat the oven to 325°F. Line a baking sheet with parchment paper and set aside. Whisk the egg whites, sugar, hot sauce, cinnamon, nutmeg, cayenne, salt, and pepper together in a large bowl. Add the pecans and toss to coat. Transfer the nuts to the prepared baking sheet and bake until they're fragrant and have a deep molasses-brown tint, 30 to 32 minutes, stirring every 8 minutes.

Remove the nuts from the oven. While the nuts are still hot and sticky, use two forks to pry them apart. Let them cool on the pan and serve immediately or store in an airtight container for up to 1 month.

MAKES 4 CUPS

Cane Syrup Snaps

Nan, my grandmother on my mom's side, always offered me two things when I came to visit: as much Dr. Pepper® as I could guzzle down and gingerbread men. They were those super-crisp, gingersnap-style gingerbread men that came in a blue tin along with sandwich cookies and coarse sugar–coated shortbread. In good form, I'd start by severing the gingerbread man's head at the neck and then eat my way through the extremities—arms, legs, and finally gobble up the torso. It didn't matter what time of year it was, because Nan always had them around, whether it was a blaring summer day or a chilly December one.

When I started to make my own gingersnaps, I called upon the spiced, sweet flavor of Nan's gingerbread men for inspiration. Instead of molasses, which can give gingersnaps a bitter edge, I like to use gentler Louisiana cane syrup. To put some pep in their step, I add some Crystal's hot sauce and a good dose of finely ground black pepper. For extra crunch and sweetness, I roll each tablespoon-size ball of dough in coarse raw sugar before baking. If you want to go for gingerbread people, you can. Let the chilled dough sit out at room temperature for 5 to 10 minutes before rolling on a well-floured work surface.

3	cups all-purpose flour plus extra for rolling
2	teaspoons baking soda
2	teaspoons finely ground black pepper
2	teaspoons ground ginger
¼	teaspoon ground cloves
½	teaspoon salt
2	sticks unsalted butter, at room temperature
1¼	cups sugar
¼	cup cane syrup
2	teaspoons hot sauce (preferably Crystal's)
1	teaspoon vanilla extract
2	large eggs
½	cup demerara or coarse brown sugar for rolling

Sift together the flour, baking soda, pepper, ginger, cloves, and salt, and set aside. Beat the butter and sugar together in the bowl of a stand mixer (or in a large bowl if using a hand mixer) until airy, about 2 minutes. Stop the mixer and pour in the cane syrup, hot sauce, and vanilla. Mix on medium-low speed until combined and then beat in the eggs, one at a time, stopping between each addition to scrape down the bottom and sides of the mixing bowl. Add the sifted dry ingredients and mix on low speed until the dough is thoroughly blended and comes together into a cohesive mass. Wrap the dough in a large sheet of plastic wrap and refrigerate for at least 2 hours or up to a couple of days (you may need to let it sit out at room temperature before using if you chill it for more than a few hours).

Heat the oven to 350°F. Place a small bowl of flour, another of demerara sugar, and a small ramekin of warm water on your work surface. Line 2 baking sheets with parchment paper and set aside.

Remove the dough from the refrigerator and unwrap. Rub a little flour between your hands (if the dough gets coated in too much flour, the sugar won't stick) and use your fingers to pull off 20 tablespoon-size knobs. Process each knob: Roll it between your hands to make a ball (flouring your hands if the dough gets sticky), roll the ball in the sugar (making sure the sugar sticks), place it on the baking sheet (space the balls about 1½ inches apart), and then dip your thumb in the warm water and press down on the center of the ball to slightly flatten it and make an indentation in its center. Fill the sheets and then bake the cookies until richly browned, 12 to 14 minutes. Remove from the oven and let cool on the sheet pan for 15 minutes before transferring to a cooling rack to cool completely. Repeat the shaping, sugaring, and baking with the remaining dough.

Store in an airtight container for up to 5 days (if you find they're getting on the soft side, you can pop them in a 350°F oven for a few minutes to re-crisp before eating).

MAKES 5 DOZEN

Caramel Peanut Popcorn

Cracker Jacks® watch out! This popcorn is so delicious I guarantee if you make it once, you'll make it again. For a more sophisticated take, try this with toasted sliced almonds instead of peanuts. Coarsely chopped pecans are delicious, too. I like to serve it up in paper cones or paper bags. It's also great bagged in cellophane and gifted away.

Caramel Peanut Popcorn

1   (3½-ounce) package plain (unbuttered natural flavor) microwave popcorn

1   cup packed light brown sugar

¼   cup light corn syrup

6   tablespoons unsalted butter, melted

¼   teaspoon salt

2   teaspoons vanilla extract

½   teaspoon baking soda

1   cup lightly salted peanuts (extra large, if available), roughly chopped

→TIP Make sure to pick out any unpopped kernels before mixing it all together. Those unpopped numbers are mighty hard!

Heat the oven to 250°F. Line a rimmed baking sheet with parchment paper and set aside.

Pop the popcorn according to the package instructions. Coat a large mixing bowl with nonstick cooking spray and transfer the popcorn from the bag to the bowl, then set the bowl aside.

Whisk the sugar, corn syrup, butter, salt, and 2 tablespoons of water in a pot and bring to a simmer over medium-high heat. Continue to simmer, stirring often, until the mixture reads 250°F on a digital thermometer, 3 to 4 minutes. Turn off the heat and whisk in the vanilla and the baking soda. Immediately pour the hot mixture over the popcorn. Use a rubber spatula to gently fold the caramel into the popcorn until all of the popcorn is coated. Gently stir in the peanuts and transfer the mixture to the prepared baking sheet. Bake for 1 hour, stirring every 20 minutes. Remove from the oven and place on a cooling rack for 20 minutes. Gently break up the popcorn and serve immediately, or store in an airtight container for up to 5 days (less if it's hot and humid).

MAKES ABOUT 10 CUPS

Turtles

I grew up surrounded by women who loved their candy. My mom had a serious soft spot for candy bars, and her bag was always littered with Milky Way® and Hundred Grand® wrappers. But her favorite candies of all were turtles, those ingenious nuggets of pecans, caramel, and chocolate. Every Valentine's Day, Easter, and during the holidays there would surely be turtles in the house. My version tastes pretty awesome, though it doesn't stand by the traditional turtle shape. Instead I stir pecans into a batch of caramel, let it set up in a baking dish, cut the caramels into squares, then dip each in melted chocolate. A more modern turtle, yes. But mom loves it all the same. For a more classic roundish shape, dip the caramels while the chocolate is still a little on the warm side. The caramel and chocolate will kind of ooze together and fuse into an amoeba-like round candy.

Turtles

1½ cups pecan pieces
1 cup heavy cream
¾ cup light corn syrup
½ cup packed light brown sugar
½ cup sugar
1 tablespoon unsalted butter
2 teaspoons vanilla extract
¼ teaspoon salt
8 ounces semisweet chocolate (preferably 58%–61% cacao)

Heat the oven to 325°F. Place the pecans on a rimmed baking sheet and roast until browned and fragrant, about 12 minutes. Remove from the oven and set aside to cool; once completely cooled, place the nuts in a gallon-size resealable plastic bag and slightly crush with a rolling pin to make smaller pieces. Set aside.

Spray an 8-inch-square baking dish with nonstick cooking spray. Fit with a piece of parchment paper long enough to fit into the bottom of the dish and hang over two opposite sides (creating parchment handles), and set the dish aside.

Place the cream, corn syrup, both sugars, and the butter in a medium saucepan over low heat. Stir often until the butter and sugar melt, using a heatproof spatula to scrape down the sides of the pan occasionally. Increase the heat to medium and continue to simmer the mixture until its temperature reads 244°F on a digital ther-mometer, 12 to 15 minutes (be careful—once the sugar hits 240°F, the temperature climbs rapidly, so stay on your toes!). If the mixture begins to bubble up to the rim of the pan, remove it from the stovetop for a second to calm the bubbles, give it a stir, and place it back on the burner. Once the caramel reaches 246°F, remove it from the heat and stir in the vanilla, salt, and pecans. Pour the mixture into the prepared baking dish and set aside in a cool spot (or refrigerator) for at least 4 hours or overnight.

Pour water into a small pot to a depth of 1 inch and simmer. Place the chocolate in a heatproof medium bowl and set it over the simmering water (the bottom of the bowl shouldn't touch the water). Reduce the heat to low and melt the choco-late, stirring often, until it's completely smooth. Pour the chocolate into a small bowl or ramekin and set aside until completely cool but still soft enough to dunk the turtles.

Run a paring knife around the edges of the baking dish and pop out the cara-mel block (see the tip on p. 161). Move to a cutting board and slice the caramel into squares between 1¼ and 1½ inches in size. Place a long sheet of parchment or waxed paper on your work surface. Dip each caramel square halfway into the chocolate, and then place on the paper to set up. After dipping, give the chocolate enough time to set up and harden, about 1 hour. Store the turtles in an airtight container in the refrigerator for up to 1 week.

MAKES ABOUT 2 DOZEN TURTLES

→TIP Here's a tasty way to test the chocolate to see if it is cool enough to make turtles: Dip a metal spoon into the melted chocolate and press it lightly on your bottom lip. If the chocolate is cool, it's ready to use; if it still feels a little warm, let it cool down more before using.

Salted Caramels

❖❖❖❖❖❖❖❖❖❖❖❖❖❖❖❖❖❖❖❖❖❖❖

My granny's purse was like a magician's bag. I'd stick my arm in shoulder blade deep and intuitively be able to sift through keys, pieces of paper, and whatnots to locate her candy. She always had a little something in there, usually either chewy caramels or butterscotch. There wasn't anything fancy about her caramels, either. They were your garden variety kind—sweet, creamy, and pull-out-your-fillings chewy. Mine are on the softer side—I like it when caramels kind of melt in your mouth. I also add a good amount of salt to my recipe because I love the contrasting tastes of sweet and salty.

❖❖❖❖❖❖❖❖❖❖❖❖❖❖❖❖❖❖❖❖❖❖❖

2 cups heavy cream

1 whole vanilla bean (prefer-ably Tahitian), split down the middle, seeds scraped from the pod and reserved

2 cups sugar

1 cup corn syrup

4 tablespoons unsalted butter, cut into small pieces

½ teaspoon salt

Spray an 8-inch-square baking dish with nonstick cooking spray. Fit with a piece of parchment paper long enough to fit into the bottom of the dish and hang over two opposite sides (creating parchment handles), and set the dish aside.

Bring the cream, vanilla seeds, and the pod to a boil in a medium saucepan. Turn off the heat, cover the pan, and set aside for 15 minutes, then strain through a fine-mesh sieve into a large measuring cup.

Stir the sugar and corn syrup together in a large pot and bring to a simmer over medium heat. Once the mixture reaches 310°F on a digital thermometer, reduce the heat to medium-low and whisk in the butter and salt. Whisk the vanilla-infused cream mixture into the hot sugar mixture in a slow and steady stream, cooking until the mixture reaches 250°F, an additional 14 to 18 minutes. (If you like softer caramels, cook the mixture only to 248°F.)

Pour the caramel into the prepared baking dish and cool for 4 hours or up to 1 day. Run a paring knife around the edges of the pan to loosen the edges and then use the parchment handles to pull and pop out the caramel block (see the tip below). Move the block to a cutting board and use a long chef's knife to slice the caramel into 1-inch squares. After slicing, wrap the caramels in brown paper candy cups or in waxed paper (not parchment paper). Stored in an airtight container, they'll keep for up to 2 weeks.

MAKES 64 CARAMELS

→TIP To easily remove the caramel from the pan for cutting (the Salted Caramels or the Turtles on p. 157), run a paring knife around the edges of the caramel in the pan. Place the baking dish directly over a low flame on your stovetop (be sure the flame is low—you don't want those parchment handles to ignite!) or on an electric coil set to low, and heat for 10 seconds at a time. This loosens the mass so you can pop it out of the pan easily and cut out squares on your cutting board rather than in the baking dish.

Peanut Brittle

I'm positive that this is the first hard candy I ever made—it's buttery and crunchy and loaded with roasted peanuts. I know this will probably be considered sacrilege, but Virginia peanuts are where it's at. Louisiana grows 'em too, but the ones from Virginia are just so big and delicious that they're the only ones I keep in the house (see pp. 167–168 for source information).

That said, you can make brittle with any kind of nut you like—I've made it with pecans, cashews, and almonds.

3   tablespoons unsalted butter, at room temperature

1½ cups lightly salted, roasted peanuts (extra-large jumbo if you can find them)

1   cup sugar

½   cup light corn syrup

1   teaspoon vanilla extract

1   teaspoon baking soda

    Pinch salt

→TIP Pulse some brittle in the food processor and sprinkle it over ice cream or even a sundae for a real treat.

Heat the oven to 325°F. Grease a silicone baking sheet, a Silpat® mat, or the back of a rimmed baking sheet with 2 tablespoons of the butter and set aside (or if you have a granite or marble countertop, lightly spray the surface with nonstick cooking spray). Line another baking sheet with parchment paper, place the peanuts on top, and roast until glossy and fragrant, 5 to 10 minutes. Remove from the oven and set aside.

Meanwhile, stir the sugar, corn syrup, and ⅓ cup of water together in a heavy-bottomed pot or large saucepan. Cook over medium-high heat until the mixture reaches 300°F. Immediately remove from the heat and, using a heatproof rubber spatula or a wooden spoon, stir in the remaining 1 tablespoon of butter, the vanilla, baking soda, salt, and peanuts (note that the mixture will become very foamy).

Immediately pour the hot mixture onto the prepared baking sheet (or countertop) and, using the spatula, spread it as thinly as possible. Cool for 30 minutes and then, using a rolling pin, the back of a metal spoon, or your hands, break the brittle into rough, craggy pieces. The brittle will keep for up to a few weeks in an airtight container.

MAKES ABOUT 1 POUND

DamGoodPicks

A Few of My Favorite Ingredients & Sources

I love being able to use ingredients from Louisiana when I can—pecans, cane syrup, hot sauce—the flavors I grew up with. I've also included some non-Louisianan favorites, because when it comes down to it, it's all about finding the best ingredients you can. If you can't find my picks, buy the best stuff available, preferably from local outfits, and above all, have fun. Good spirits are perhaps the most important ingredient of all.

ABITA ROOT BEER

Craft-brewed 30 miles north of New Orleans, caffeine-free Abita root beer is made with spring water from Abita, herbs, vanilla, and yucca for foam, and is sweetened with Louisiana cane sugar instead of corn syrup. Distributed to 33 states, Abita is worth searching out, especially if you're going to make the Sweet Corn Cake with Root Beer Syrup on p. 76. Abita is available online at www.nolacajun.com.

BUTTER

I bake with unsalted butter. When a recipe calls for room-temperature butter, it means that the butter should be soft enough to cream without worrying about lumps. The stick should still be waxy and hold its shape well—if it has a sheen to it and starts to deflate, it's too warm. My absolute favorite to bake with is Plugra®, a delicious high-fat European-style butter with great tanginess.

CANE SYRUP

Steen's Cane Syrup is my go-to brand when it comes to this thick, syrupy molasses-like sweetener. It is made near my Aunt Boo's house in Abbeville from Louisiana sugarcane boiled in an open kettle until rich and dark. You can find it in grocery stores or online at www.steensyrup.com.

CHANTILLY CREAM

Heavy cream, sugar, and a splash of vanilla extract all whipped together into airy peaks—this is chantilly cream. I use confectioners' sugar to make mine a little more stable. The finished product doesn't weep as much, meaning you can make it up to an hour or two ahead and keep it in the fridge before serving. Give it a stir before dolloping. See the recipe on p. 53.

CHOCOLATE

My favorite all-purpose readily available chocolate is from San Francisco's E. Guittard®. The disk-style wafers come in one-pound boxes and are available through many supermarkets (I get mine at my local Safeway℠). The small disks make melting the chocolate easy. In addition, if a recipe calls for chopped chocolate, a few rough chops with a chef's knife get the job done. If you're looking for something really nuanced and decadent, go ahead and splurge for Valrhona®, a wonderful French-made chocolate with great acidity.

The percentage of cacao you often see tagged onto a variety refers to the amount of pure cacao in the chocolate. More cacao means more intense chocolate flavor and less sugar. I go for Guittard's 72% bittersweet when I'm looking for a complex, slightly bitter, edgy flavor. It works really well in super decadent desserts because it helps to counter sweetness and richness. I use the 72% bittersweet in the chocolate bread pudding on p. 16 and in the peanut-butter brownies on p. 78. When I'm looking for a sweeter, classic chocolatey taste, I go for Guittard's 62% semisweet. It's excellent in the Chocolate Chip Cookie Cake on p. 65 and my chocolate pudding on p. 95. You can order it online at www.guittard.com.

COCOA POWDER

There are two kinds of cocoa powder: Dutch processed and natural. Both are derived from dried cocoa liquor, a compressed cake made from cocoa beans after they've been fermented, dried, roasted, and rid of fatty cocoa butter (one of the main ingredients in white chocolate). The liquor gets further ground into powder, hence, cocoa powder. When the natural ground powder is treated with an alkali to neutralize its acidity, it is referred to as Dutch-processed cocoa. Dutched cocoa has a darker color and a more mellow flavor than natural cocoa, which is why I choose to use Dutch-processed cocoa in my recipes. If the label doesn't indicate whether the cocoa is Dutched or not, a good rule to follow (which of course has its exceptions) is that many European cocoas like Valrhona are Dutched, while domestic brands, like Ghirardelli®, are left au naturel.

COFFEE

French roast coffee is fairly dark roasted, though not as dark as Italian roast beans (also sometimes called "espresso roast"). Ideally, the beans should contribute a rich and bold but not bitter flavor. I've tested many brands of coffee in my Café au Lait Crème Brûlée (p. 100) and discovered a couple of favorites: the Santa Lucia® brand (www.santaluciacoffee.com) and Community Coffee French roast (www.communitycoffee.com). Try to avoid super dark, charred-smelling beans, as they lend an astringent quality to the custard.

COFFEE AND CHICORY

Coffee and chicory go back to the Civil War, when coffee beans were scarce; to extend their coffee supply, New Orleanians ground their coffee beans with dried chicory root. With a flavor that is big and bold, coffee and chicory are a must for a New Orleans–style café au lait. There are a bunch of brands I like, my favorite being good ol' Community Coffee. French Market and Café du Monde are great, too, and more widely available. You can find them all at www.nolacajun.com.

CRYSTAL HOT SAUCE

Milder than Tabasco®, Crystal's is made from ground and aged cayenne peppers, vinegar, and salt near New Orleans in Reserve, Louisiana. The company used to be right in the city on Tulane Avenue but had to move its operation (three million gallons per year!) due to damage sustained by Katrina. It's available in most grocery stores, as well as in 75 countries. I love adding a shake to my Gâteau de Sirop (p. 73), Spiced Pecans (p. 150), and Cane Syrup Snaps (p. 152).

EGGS

Always large, always fresh. I get mine from the farmers' market when possible.

FLOUR

I call for three kinds of flour: all-purpose, bread, and White Lily. Flour has varying protein levels that depend on the kind of wheat it was made from—hard or soft. Hard wheat yields stronger flour, great for breads and my beignets. Soft wheat is what you want for tender biscuits.

When it comes to all-purpose, which is often a blend of hard and soft wheat, I always use unbleached and unbromated because it has a cleaner flavor. All-purpose is exactly that, all-purpose and perfect for a variety of recipes from cakes to cookies and quick breads. Some all-purpose flours, like King Arthur®, Heckers®, and Ceresota®, have a protein content between all-purpose flour and bread flour. If you're using such a high-protein all-purpose, use 1 to 2 tablespoons less of the flour for every 1 cup of flour called for to make up for the added strength.

Bread flour contains more gluten because it is milled from harder wheat. It's great for baked goods that need to be kneaded, like my beignets (p. 6). The developed gluten acts as a net to trap in air generated by yeast; without the strong net, you wouldn't get as high of a rise or as many air pockets.

White Lily is in a genre all its own. Milled exclusively from soft wheat, it has a very low protein content and is a necessity in my biscuits (p. 137). If using White Lily in place of regular all-purpose, be sure to add 2 tablespoons of extra flour for every 1 cup of flour called for. You can find this brand in supermarkets in the Mid-Atlantic, Midwest, and South, or online at www.onlinestore.smucker.com.

HERBSAINT

Herbsaint is a neon yellow anise-flavored liqueur invented in New Orleans soon after Prohibition was repealed in the 1930s. After absinthe was vilified and outlawed for its use of wormwood (and green fairies), Herbsaint became the required ingredient for the Sazerac cocktail, America's first cocktail, invented by Antoine Peychaud, a French Quarter pharmacist. Made from brandy, Herbsaint, a dash of bitters, a sugar cube, and a lemon peel, the Sazerac isn't the only famous Herbsaint-influenced dish. Ever heard of oysters Rockefeller? Yep, the real deal has Herbsaint in it, too. You can find it in liquor shops or online for about $20.

HONEY

Honey comes in lots of shades and flavors depending on the kinds of flowers the bees collected pollen from, from buckwheat to blueberry, star thistle to sage. In my cupboard, I most often have a large jar of clover and buckwheat honey that I buy from Gunter's, a cooperative honey outfit that blends and bottles in

Berryville, Virginia. Clover and wildflower honeys have that classic honey bear flavor, while buckwheat honey is deeper and stronger with a malty tinge—it's what I use in my Fig Jam (p. 130). Sourwood or basswood honeys would also work great. There are loads of single-origin artisanal honeys being made that highlight honey from one type of blossom. You can likely find them at your farmers' market, at gourmet shops, or online. Two great sources are www.savannahbee.com and www.beeraw.com.

MAKER'S MARK BOURBON

Bourbon's sweetness and its caramelly-mellow-toasty flavor are at home with desserts like my Sweet Corn Cake with Root Beer Syrup (p. 76) and Bourbon-Chocolate Chip Pecan Pie (p. 38). Still made in Kentucky in small batches, Maker's hand-dipped red wax–topped bottle signifies a long-standing southern tradition of craftsmanship and taste.

NEW ORLEANS NECTAR SODA SYRUP

Invented in the late 19th century by pharmacy chemists, cherry-red nectar soda syrup was New Orleans' very own soda fountain invention. Back in the day, you could go to K & B, our local drugstore, waltz up to the soda fountain counter, and order a nectar cream soda: 1 tablespoon of cream to 6 ounces of nectar soda over ice. It's also a popular flavoring for sno-balls. I love it with club soda and ice cream, like a root beer float (but better!). See the recipe on p. 112. If you don't happen to live in Louisiana or one of the other few states where it's sold, you can buy it online at www.beveragesdirect.com.

NUTS

Of course I'm partial to Louisiana pecans (see p. 39 for more information), but when it comes to peanuts, I'm all about Virginia jumbos by Balducci's® (available at www.balduccis.com). Either way, I almost always toast nuts before using them, even when they're going to be baked again, as in the almond-topped berry crumble on p. 48. Toasting them slowly, for about 15 minutes, at 350°F brings out their oils and enhances their flavor. Toasted nuts really make a recipe. For smaller batches of nuts, you can toast them stovetop in a skillet over low heat, stirring every couple of minutes until they're toasty and brown.

PECTIN

Because I don't like my jams too sweet or too jelled for that matter, I like to use pure pectin. Most often made from apples, pure ground pectin is available online and in health-food stores (it's often used as a fiber supplement). If you can't find it, a widely available alternative is Pomona's® pure citrus pectin. A box of it comes with a packet of monocalcium phosphate that is used to activate the pectin—you need to dissolve the monocalcium phosphate and add it to the fruit along with the pectin. Follow the box instructions for amounts and substitutions. Apple pectin powder can be purchased online at www.amazon.com, and Pomona's can be ordered at www.pomonapectin.com.

SALT

In this book when I call for salt, I mean table salt. Its small grains are easy to work into a mix, batter, or dough, and most everyone has it in their kitchen. That said, I often bake with kosher salt since it's what I cook with most often. If you like using kosher too, double the amount of salt called for in a recipe if using Diamond Crystal® kosher salt. If you're using Morton's® kosher salt, which has smaller salt crystals, increase the quantity by only one-half.

I'm a big fan of finishing a dessert with flaky salt like Maldon® or fleur de sel from Brittany. It works especially well with a chocolate dessert or one that toes the line of savory, like buttery crêpes (p. 20).

SUGAR

In addition to granulated sugar (I prefer sugar made from sugarcane rather than sugar beets), I use light and dark brown sugar as well as demerara sugar. Light and dark brown sugars are, at their essence, simply granulated plus molasses—less for light brown sugar and more for dark brown. If you live in a cool, dry climate, store your opened brown sugar in a resealable plastic bag so it doesn't harden. Demerara is a coarse, crunchy brown sugar that lends a great sugary crunch to the Cane Syrup Snaps on p. 152 and the Café au Lait Crème Brûlée on p. 100. It's a more flavorful version of the turbinado sugar in Sugar in the Raw® packets you can get in coffee shops. If your supermarket doesn't sell bagged demerara or my second choice, turbinado (works just as well, texturally speaking), stock up on those sugar packets and you're good to go. A great online resource is www.chefshop.com. They have all kinds of brown sugar, as well as Steen's cane syrup and Tahitian vanilla beans.

VANILLA

When it comes to vanilla, I'm a fan of Tahitian through and through. Its flowery essence and tropical flavor is light and accommodating (see p. 91 for more on Tahitian vanilla). Nothing beats vanilla beans in ice cream and custard, with their speckles adding texture as well as that soft vanilla taste. Again, here I prefer Tahitian vanilla beans, but they can be hard to find, so in a pinch I do buy beans from Madagascar. Whole beans are expensive, so buy them wisely. Look for plump beans with a waxy appearance. If the bean looks thin and dry, leave it on the shelf. Nielsen Massey® is a brand name I trust when it comes to vanilla. They sell through www.surlatable.com. Chefshop.com sells Tahitian beans, too.

EQUIVALENCY CHARTS

LIQUID/DRY MEASURES

U.S.	Metric
¼ teaspoon	1.25 milliliters
½ teaspoon	2.5 milliliters
1 teaspoon	5 milliliters
1 tablespoon (3 teaspoons)	15 milliliters
1 fluid ounce (2 tablespoons)	30 milliliters
¼ cup	60 milliliters
⅓ cup	80 milliliters
½ cup	120 milliliters
1 cup	240 milliliters
1 pint (2 cups)	480 milliliters
1 quart (4 cups; 32 ounces)	960 milliliters
1 gallon (4 quarts)	3.84 liters
1 ounce (by weight)	28 grams
1 pound	454 grams
2.2 pounds	1 kilogram

OVEN TEMPERATURES

°F	Gas Mark	°C
250	½	120
275	1	140
300	2	150
325	3	165
350	4	180
375	5	190
400	6	200
425	7	220
450	8	230
475	9	240
500	10	260
550	Broil	290

Index